PERSONALITY
AND
LEADERSHIP BEHAVIOR

HENRY P. KNOWLES / BORJE O. SAXBERG

University of Washington

ADDISON-WESLEY PUBLISHING COMPANY

Reading, Massachusetts · Menlo Park, California · London · Don Mills, Ontario

This book is in the

ADDISON-WESLEY SERIES IN SOCIAL SCIENCE AND ADMINISTRATION

under the editorship of Warren G. Bennis

To Claudia, Vivi, and colleagues

PREFACE

We explore in this book the human relationships which link individuals together, for better or worse, in our organizational society. The emphasis is on those facilitating interpersonal processes which arise, not from bureaucratic structures, from procedures and rules, from the paper flow across a desk, or from budgets and financial appropriations, but from the day-in and day-out common stuff of human experience. Each of us, regardless of the particular context, be it the family, the business firm, the university, the church, the government agency, or whatever the setting may be, inescapably faces the social, the face-to-face dimensions of an organizational environment. In the process we affect and are affected by those with whom we associate in terms of feelings, emotions, attitudes, and values.

Early in this book we outline the influence of ideas about the nature of man himself, on a number of systems of social control—in economics, in biology, in politics, in psychotherapy, and in organizational life. How individuals and persons in society look at human nature is basic to interpersonal behavior. We then expand upon this theme, first, by tracing the evolution of human values as a product of personality development, and second, by showing their effect on interpersonal relationships. Later, we introduce into our discussion the means by which such values can be examined and changed. The underlying theme which emerges is a model for supportive and adaptive leadership. We believe such leadership is essential in a world of change where control through communication and cooperation is beginning to seriously challenge traditional leadership styles.

This book represents our concern that with the increasing emphasis on material values in a society of affluence, sight may be lost of the intrinsic humanity which is required in order for society to survive. Man walks a path of snags and quicksand which, often without his knowing it, are there to trap him or to induce him into trapping others. But his course must, wherever possible, be left behind with some of these pitfalls overcome, others dodged, but none as his fate. We can be accused of taking an overly optimistic, even a naive view of man. Let it be clear that our position is deliberately taken because we believe that there is a need to emphasize the best in human relationships. We see the role of the manager, the administrator, or the authority figure as one of strategic importance because such a person is in a position to mold organizational relationships. He does this by the example he sets through his judgments, decisions, and the values they reflect. He faces the challenge of creating conditions of supportive cooperation, of bringing about collaborative action in which his personal efforts and those of his associates add up to a synergism, that is, to something more than the sum of individual contributions.

We draw heavily on materials from sociology, psychology, cultural anthropology, and the clinical sciences, on knowledge gained from research and from extensive experience in university classrooms, management consulting, and executive training programs. One of our objectives in these activities has been to help managers and students of management to increase their awareness of themselves and their sensitivity to the needs and feelings of others. In these areas, our approach has been clinical before being theoretical, pragmatic rather than speculative. We are also indebted to the works of many behavioral scientists whose names will be found in the bibliography at the end of this book. We express to them our appreciation for their contributions to science, and absolve them from any misinterpretations we may inadvertently have made.

The material in this volume has been tested in studies and course work in human relations, organizational behavior, and human aspects of administration in schools and graduate schools of business, education, public administration, librarianship, nursing, and social work, as well as in management development programs in industry and government. In all these contexts, the material in this book has been used to complement experiential training activity involving case studies, role-playing, and sensitivity training. This volume should also be highly useful to any layman who is puzzled about man and the nature of man, and the factors which influence his personality formation as he progresses on his life arch. No man can afford in today's world to neglect the opportunity to explore his own personality, to make a serious attempt to understand himself and others, and to apply this information to all his human encounters in constructive ways.

We would like to express our appreciation to the staff at Addison-Wesley Publishing Company. We are also grateful to our reviewers, in particular, to Warren Bennis, for their helpful comments and suggestions.

August 1970   H. P. K.
Seattle, Washington   B. O. S.

CONTENTS

CHAPTER ONE

INTRODUCTION

"The cardinal problem of our time . . . is the pathology of the normal group."

J. L. MORENO

Competence in interpersonal relations has become an important goal of American managers and business leaders. By interpersonal relations we mean the whole range of human conduct between individuals who interact as they are involved in relationships of communicating, cooperating, changing, problem-solving, and motivating. More and more, managers are attending executive development programs, human relations courses, sensitivity training sessions, and behavioral symposia, seeking the elusive key to more effective relationships with colleagues and subordinates. At the same time, interest has broadened from the traditional personnel management base to the all-inclusive field of organizational development. No longer is the foreman-employee relationship of primary concern. Equal emphasis is now given to superior-subordinate and peer relationships in the higher echelons, including those in top management, as executives now recognize that "human relations" for the masses simply does not work if there are "unhuman relations" among members of the organizational elite.

This concern with interpersonal relations in business and industry as well as in other organizations, appears at a time when many sectors of society are experiencing a transition from traditional values to a new morality and ethic. The revolt of students in colleges and universities across the land, the demands of black men for equal rights, and the frustrations of war are symptomatic of an upheaval in many of our social values. Students protest against the monolithic culture of the academic "factory" where administrators enforce impersonal rules and members of the faculty avoid students wherever possible in order to conserve time to "publish or perish." Black men describe themselves as "souls on ice"—objects that have been methodically stripped of their humanity by an indifferent white society. Hawk and dove together stand in frustrated helplessness as the "most unwanted war" grinds impersonally forward toward no one knows what end.

These crises all seem to have a common denominator. They arise from the frustrations and anxieties that occur when the individual comes finally to the conclusion that he, as he experiences himself, counts for little before the massive and irresistible power of the Establishment or the Syndicate or the Organization. To compensate for this, he seeks an outlet in the form of aggressive action against the symbols of impersonal power—in the cases we have cited, the college administrator, the white society, the war industries and the ROTC. Behavior may also take other forms: withdrawal from the reaches of power, as in the case of the employee who quits his job in rebellion against oppressive authority, or, what may be worse, automaton conformity to the wishes of those in power. Automaton conformity, to whatever degree it is present, reduces by that much the individual's capacity to respond as a unique, contributing person. Whatever abilities he may have, whatever creative ideas may exist as seeds in his mind, whatever he may have of himself to give, is lessened to the extent that conditions have precluded the development of free and constructive relationships with others.

In addition to this alienation from society and its work, a man may, through inhibitions stemming from poor interpersonal relationships, become alienated from himself. This kind of alienation leads to an incapacity to communicate effectively with others, ineffectual cooperation, indiscriminate use of force or cowardly retreat, resistance to change, and, in some cases, mental illness in some form of neurosis.

The world crisis in human relationships has not overlooked the organizational society, the flesh and blood of modern industrial civilization. Though outwardly calm and efficient, the corporation is inwardly troubled. Executive talent, concerned with achievement, a plentiful resource in years gone by, is getting harder and harder to find. Many bright young men, disillusioned by the traditional business image cast up on Madison Avenue and in trading marts both at home and abroad, hold higher expectations in regard to the quality of their contributions to society than employment in business. This type of expectation has, up until now, more often been associated with a life in government service or the professions.

Perhaps the most dramatic symptom of crisis in the human aspects of administration, the strike or walkout by organized employees in a critical industry, is of less immediate concern, since it has long been visible as a symptom, and routines for reducing its effects have been worked out. The underlying disease, however, is harder to get at because it finally reduces to the least understood of human problems—man against man, and man against himself. The subtle and powerful effects of psychological maladies on organizational health are the more threatening to management because they are not susceptible to traditional engineering and accounting methods of analysis and are, therefore, difficult to diagnose and to treat.

In this book we shall look at problems at the interpersonal level, the level which involves man's nature and personality and the quality of the relationships which emerge between men when they work together as organizational members. We shall concern ourselves with face-to-face relationships where human understanding, feelings, and control are involved. We shall, in fact, explore the managerial mind as it relates to the manager's function as a leader. His concept of the kind of person he is and ought to be is of singular importance.

THE ORGANIZATIONAL TRADITION

As we think of membership in an organization, we are generally hidebound by the legacy of the Industrial Revolution and the beliefs underlying the Protestant Ethic. We assume that man, as a responsible individual, has a duty to give his best to his work and his organization in order to provide sustenance for himself and his family and to live a healthy, normal existence. The role of theoretician for the business firm in those early years of industrial development was played by the classical economist. The economist emphasized the cost-revenue relationship in his formulations and recommendations to management. Thus, management came to regard labor as a commodity cost. This combination of the Protestant Ethic and classical economics was implicit in the employment contract which provided that the company, in return for a promise to pay the wages required by the conditions of the labor market, had the full effort and spirit of the employee at its disposal—his body and soul.

The overtones of these attitudes are recognizable in the early writings of Fredrick W. Taylor on scientific management. At the turn of the century Taylor was an influential proponent of work methods and cost efficiency. He assumed that the firm could reach its objectives and goals of productive performance only when it could achieve the most favorable cost-efficiency ratio. Thus, he believed that management's attention must focus on labor's economic performance. The employee was in effect regarded as an instrument which the organization could use to achieve its objectives and goals. Taylor advised management that the employee would adjust any personal goals and needs sufficiently to accommodate himself to the requirements of the task at hand. Accordingly, Taylor proposed that management should (1) specify performance requirements and precise work methods for the employee and enforce these requirements and (2) provide the incentive by making financial rewards proportional to productive output.

We see the same kind of reasoning in Max Weber's work on bureaucracy. Max Weber, a well-known nineteenth-century German sociologist and student of organization, assumed that man was an irrational component of organization. He based his theories on the premise that an organization must be capable of achieving its objectives and goals in spite of this element of irrationality. In this, Weber agrees with the position of Taylor. He looked at the organization from top management's point of view, and designed a rational organizational structure and various structural sub-parts based on the objectives and goals to be reached. Again, in relation to the organization, man was reduced to an instrument by means of hierarchical authority relationships, written procedures and rules, and precise position descriptions. In this manner, Weber hoped to minimize or eliminate from organizational life independent, unpredictable, and irrational human behavior governed by feelings and emotions and substitute therefor rational calculation and predictable human performance.

In fact, even the human relations movement under Elton Mayo and the work done by him and his associates at the Hawthorne plant of the Western Electric Company in the 1920's and early 30's has been labeled as the work of handmaidens to management. The focal point of the investigations at Hawthorne, a landmark research which laid the groundwork for modern organizational psychology, concerned the means by which managers could increase productivity mainly by motivating employees to cooperation at work. However, the investigators clearly held a value bias that human behavior at work, including productive performance, was related to the accompanying social conditions in the plant. Moreover, Elton Mayo himself based his viewpoint on the value premise that man has become lost and alienated in the urban, industrialized world. Therefore, in addition to looking for the causes of employee behavior in the social conditions at work, Mayo called upon management to provide man with a work community characterized by levels of security and personal satisfaction. Mayo assumed that these conditions would correspond to the desirable work environment of an earlier era of rural village community life.

MANAGERIAL LAG

We have sketched the historical development of management attitudes toward the employee as a reflection of the environmental conditions and the social values of the times. We must also point to the inevitability of *managerial lag* as a factor in perpetuating these values. Managers in their leadership and behavior are reluctant to take radical steps beyond what they learned from those under whom they trained. Managerial behavior and attitudes tend, therefore, to reflect those of a past generation and be permanently out of step with the requirements of the present. Only where managers are willing to recognize the obsolescence of traditional attitudes and make a deliberate attempt to revise their approach, do we see a narrowing in this gap.

Our nation has experienced a tremendous increase in productivity as a result of technological development and increasing managerial sophistication in the use of new machines and equipment. Simultaneously, in its concern about man, society as a whole has progressed beyond the idea that he should merely accept responsibility for a contribution to the material output of society. As a result, the benefits of improved productivity have not been in terms of increased wages alone. They also include a saving in *time*, part of which has been devoted to further education and part to an increase in leisure time. We now deal with new generations of employees with new expectations and new aspirations. In today's affluent society, employees expect a wide range of alternatives to satisfy their personal objectives and goals. In the past we assumed that man's mental health was related mainly to his being engaged in work. Under present conditions we find that society considers leisure or free time also essential in maintaining mental health.

In the past we tended to think of managers and professionals as being involved in a situation where work and life coincide and where, therefore, a distinction between work and free time or leisure was irrelevant. However, we know that nobody in today's world, not the church, nor the state, nor the business firm, nor their leaders and members can escape the transition in values taking place in society. Increasingly, society holds up the concept of the whole man pursuing a relevant balance between the needs of his spirit, his mind, and his body as preferable to the former image of ideal man driven in a single-minded pursuit of personal material success.

As society has accepted the idea that man's life has more meaning than just to subsist on a physical level or be an instrument of the business organization, the concept of man as an end in himself has emerged as a matter of vital concern. We may speculate that existential philosophy with its basic assumption that man's existence in and of itself is of critical importance has more relevance today than the Protestant Ethic. Be that as it may, this era of affluence allows each individual a greater amount of discretionary decision-making and choice than ever before. The traditional demands for conformity to conventions, rules, and mores are regarded as absurd by many members of the new generation, and there is now a deliberate concern for man's potentialities, his temporality, and his eventual death. As a result of these changes in the societal fabric of values, organizations are experiencing a critical confrontation with new generations of members who expect that their personal objectives and goals will be regarded by the organizational hierarchy as worthwhile and important.

Developments in the behavioral sciences since the time of Mayo have provided managers with means for the manipulative adjustment of members to organizational objectives and goals. Unfortunately, these developments have most often been applied where the prevailing point of view has been that man *is an instrument of the organization* and can be adapted to the organization's needs and purposes. More and more, however, we perceive a need for assurance that the relationship between managers and managed at interpersonal levels will be characterized by feelings of consideration and mutual acceptance. The viewpoint advocated here is that *the organization is an instrument of man,* and therefore the quality of interpersonal relations among its members is critical not only for organizational success but also in order that organization may best serve the needs and thus the development and efficiency of man.

We find this idea carried through in the acceptance by management of concepts of organizational development including sensitivity training or t-group training as a vehicle for introducing planned change in organizations. This approach involves not only structural and technological change, but change in the people concerned as well. Such training is uniquely defined in terms of changing the social environment in the direction of democratization of organizations. For this purpose we find that organization planning departments exist side by side with organization development departments with "change in people" deliberately incorporated as an important part in planning.

HUMAN UNDERSTANDING ESSENTIAL

Against this background, an understanding of the employee at work as a representative of mankind engaged in industrial pursuit becomes both worthwhile and critical. Increasingly we need to concentrate on and emphasize the potentialities of man in a wide range of activities, the most important of which are still within the world of work. Leaders need a deeper understanding of man's nature as it is measured and defined in the dimensions of his personality if they are to evaluate intelligently opportunities within the organization which will allow each of its members to realize his fullest potential. Leaders must also be aware that the realization of this potential may take place at work or outside work. Managerial leadership must increasingly be concerned with its responsibility to provide opportunities for individual development. In this scheme of things, man becomes important as an end in himself, and the leaders and the led improve their chances to accommodate each other's objectives and goals in a mutually satisfactory way.

These considerations shed new light on the importance of the human aspects of administration. We are faced with answering the normative question: What ought to be the governing rule in interpersonal relations? As we have pointed out previously, the criterion for industry has been and still remains *effectiveness* in meeting the needs of the organization and its members. In the past, effectiveness has frequently been equated with personal gain. In this new and rapidly changing age this is not enough if human potentials are to be reached. We must now begin to think in terms of total human effectiveness in the organizational setting.

Organizational relationships place boundaries upon the behavior of those confined within the operational unit. Certain constraints are imposed by others on the members of the organization. Definition of position and organizational role, time schedules, and objectives may be crucial for the survival of the organization. Frequently, however, organizational constraints become superfluous or ends in themselves but continue to exist through a lack of continuing review by management. They might include, for example, the degree of supervision and the rules and procedures under which the organization is assumed to operate. In some cases, we find organizational constraints that are actually detrimental to the survival of the organization. Such constraints may occur in atomistic work relationships, lack of informal roles, and in the neglect of the potential in the total work environment and in the creativity of the individuals working there singly or collectively.

DEFICIENCY IN INTERPERSONAL RELATIONS

Science has shown the way in man's mastery of his environment. Through the application of the scientific method all the forces and all the alternatives are brought forth. Accomplishing this creative, challenging task on a continuing basis cannot, however, take place within the organizational setting except where interpersonal relations are of a high order. Where the climate of leadership becomes too fixed, too authoritarian, too production-oriented, thought processes are strangled and unable to cope with the demands of changing conditions.

It is our observation that, for the conditions of our time, interpersonal relationships are at a low level in business and industry generally. Although change is demanded by a changing world of social, economic, and political conditions, change meets resistance. Change encounters friction which interferes with organizational progress. But this resistance to change is not a natural human phenomenon. Man's survival through time is a testimony to his resiliency, his capacity for adaptation and change. Resistance to change develops through fear of unknown consequences and threats to personal security. Much of this fear stems from inadequate, parsimonious interpersonal relationships which encourage material competition but provide personal and moral support for no one. As a result, physical, technological, and financial considerations have historically outweighed—indeed, in some cases, have denied—the importance of human relations to economic and social progress. This has been occurring in spite of the widespread programs in "human relations in industry" during the past twenty or thirty years.

An improvement in economic, educational, and social conditions has transformed our society into a new society. As we move into the future, those who are the strong today may be the weak tomorrow, given a base of social mobility and an ideology which encourages the development of an open society and status attained by achievement. Traditionally, we have been accustomed to the idea that in any organizational situation there will develop a stable class and a stable power relationship between the elite and the masses, the manager and the managed. But we need to recognize that, in fact, in the relationship between the employer and the employee, the foreman and the machinist, or the department head and the section chief, the subordinate may on many occasions be superior to his boss because of specialized knowledge, presence of mind in a crisis, thinking ability, or some other quality.

The relationship between the elite and the masses, or leader and follower should, therefore, be open and flexible rather than closed and fixed, and it should be allowed to change with the requirements of the situation if the organization and society are to draw the maximum benefits from it.

Buber has suggested that "man is good and he is bad." Man, therefore, needs to exercise constant vigil over the direction of his development. He can by means of self-control encourage the good and check the bad, as defined by the values of society's institutions, values that change with time and situation. To move freely in this way, the individual must be shown respect as a whole man rather than for the particular functional task he happens to be engaged in for the moment. Creating and maintaining such an atmosphere calls for empathy on the part of all who are involved—managers and managed, leaders and led—empathy in the sense of being sensitive to the needs and desires of others and empathy as reflected in behavior based upon a humanistic conviction. This calls for relationships based on cooperation rather than acquiescence, influence rather than power, and communication rather than lack of insight into the views of others.

Through management's sensitivity to the significant interpersonal environment, individuals can be released from constraints. They can be motivated to reach for greater heights of personal development and performance—to actualize themselves—if they feel that institutional goals are relevant to their own objectives and goals. The individual and the organization, the employee and the employer, are in need of each other. Neither can accomplish goals and objectives without the other. Increased awareness of the other's humanity and aspirations can effect a change in interpersonal relationships that will lead to better performance and individual growth and development. The old arrangement in which the managed are instruments of the manager will give way to a mutuality in which each works to the advantage of the other.

Our objective, then, is to emphasize the fact that the worker and management, junior executive and senior, require each other and benefit by a mutual accommodation of objectives and goals. Man as a human being is constantly undergoing change through development and growth. In the past, this development and growth may have been frustrated and submerged in the interests of the organization's objectives and goals. Today the organization more often serves to enhance man's potential and enables him to reach fulfillment. To the extent that we have, in the world of work, the opportunity for the emerging of open personalities, to that extent we have a base on which to develop a social and cultural working environment characterized by a high content of information and viable interpersonal relationships. These in turn increase the capacity of business institutions to develop into open organizations, adaptive to changes in their environment. At the same time, the general degree of dependency on power relationships can be reduced and the organization as a whole can move toward professionalism in the highest sense of that word.

The organization as an organic system, is dynamic. Interplays among its members lead constantly to internal change, even as change impinges from the outside. Even though it might be possible to define change analytically in categories of technical change, job task change, cultural change, and so on, we know from experience that no change can be confined to one dimension only. Inevitably, a change always involves the total environment in all its varied facets. Thus, our effort here reflects a concern for providing a self-fulfilling cycle for man at work, as well as for the work organization of which he is a part.

Since we need new dimensions of human achievement in organizational life today, we must seek new ways of relating to one another. We need to become more aware of ourselves and more sensitive to other people. We need to improve our skills in listening and in communicating, in diagnosing human situations, and in the planning and implementation of change. We must, in short, seek to raise the level of interpersonal relations in the working world.

As a society, we achieved a position of world supremacy in the industrial sciences and arts under the philosophy and methods of the Industrial Revolution. But we now must face the fact that that era is over, and we have passed into another time where change is creating new kinds of problems which can no longer be solved with old ideas and principles. In the new technological age, all men, manager and managed alike, must be free to respond and grow and realize their human potential in the service of mankind.

SOME ELEMENTS OF INTERPERSONAL RELATIONS

Interpersonal relations, as we know, refers to the thoughts and behavior of individuals as they interact with each other. In organizational settings, personal and task objectives are nearly always found together, sometimes with emphasis on task, sometimes on the satisfaction of personal needs. In all these processes, each person is both subject and object. He has certain thoughts which are private and subjective; i.e., he is feeling something, he is wishing or wanting something. At the same time, he may be voicing certain words and carrying out certain activities which, to an observer, are interpreted as "He is saying something," "He is doing something."

Seeing another as an object means that we are inclined to take him at face value and base our interaction with him on what we observe him to be doing or what we hear him to be saying. We rarely ever speculate concerning those aspects of him which are hidden from view. This lack of analysis has certain advantages. Accepting only what we observe about another gives us direct evidence concerning the nature of his activity. By comparing this with our past experience in similar situations we can explain what we see and make predictions about what may happen next. In this process, we can seek guidance from scientific generalizations about human behavior which, at least in terms of probability, are useful and true. "Seeing is believing" is a "common sense" posture to take in our dealings with others. However, since we overlook any inner choices the other person makes, we are apt to assume that as an organism he simply reacts to his environment, robot-like, and that as a consequence only outside influences are important. We can avoid dealing with the subjective aspects of his person which seem threatening or distasteful to us—his anger, for example, or his anxieties and feelings. "Leave your personal sentiments out of this!" Or "I want an objective answer, Sherwood!" Having drawn the curtain on thoughts we do not want to hear, we need not be troubled with alien and perhaps uncomfortable ideas.

Seeing another as a subject means that we are concerned with his thoughts and feelings, with his actual substance and his potentialities as distinguished from his outward qualities and attributes. This point of view may lead us to ignore society's conventions and rules and to revere individual freedom and choice to the exclusion of the collective wisdom of others. It may also lead to an over-concern with motives and the basis for them—to the virtual exclusion of manifest behavior and its consequences. On the other hand, concern for another's essential individuality has some advantages. It opens up a source of information about another person which would not otherwise be available. It enables us to learn something about his hopes and fears, permitting us to help him achieve or avoid them. We cannot help another person achieve his potential capacity to act unless we know what he needs. We cannot know him nor can we cooperate effectively with him—nor he with us—unless we are concerned with his uniqueness and are acquainted with his personal capacities and he with ours.

Some people take an instrumental view of human nature and have a tendency to treat themselves and others as objects, as tools, as things, as parts in a material culture. Other people emphasize a subjective view and are more concerned with feelings, inner experiences, and the fulfillment of personal capacities and potentialities. Competence in interpersonal relations involves the capacity to view ourselves and others in both dimensions. If we cannot see ourselves in the minds of others we cannot respond appropriately to the image they have of us. This kind of understanding requires that we speculate about the subjective side of their nature. At the same time, without such speculation to add to the evidence of our eyes and ears, we cannot always respond appropriately to what we see and hear.

Viewing man as an object can tell us how, as an organism, he responds to social pressures and controls, but we must think of him also as a subject operating in the personal world of values, attitudes, and ideals. Only then can we expect him to have a responsibility for and an identification with needs of the organization and of society.

COMMUNICATION, COOPERATION, AND CHANGE

Certain interpersonal processes that are of critical importance in face-to-face relationships will be discussed in this book. These are communication, cooperation, and change. Of these, perhaps no human skill is more important and less clearly understood than communication, i.e., transmitting ideas, directions, orders, and so on, through the written or spoken word modified by the inevitable silent language of sentiments, gestures, tone, and expression. These modifications are often more important and more meaningful than the words themselves. Often subtle, they may augment clarity and understanding from the viewpoint of either the sender or receiver or both; they may, however, bring distortions which defeat meanings or totally disrupt the process and block any exchange of imformation at all.

Closely related to and dependent upon communication is the cooperative process. In a society in which division of labor ranges from the differentiated but highly interdependent roles of male and female to the less complex sharing of work in a modern factory or service organization, cooperation is a basic instrument of interpersonal relations. Too often we tend to view cooperation as a simple power relationship or as a unilateral manipulation in which one person "motivates" another. Cooperation, however, has to be more of a mutual relationship than this if each person or group involved is to give fully in achieving a shared goal. It requires joint action to ensure that complementary knowledge and skills are combined and applied in a common effort.

Similarly, change—the alteration of personal attitudes, values, or goals in either or both parties involved in a relationship—has an important bearing on both communication and the cooperative process. Getting another to cooperate may require that one or both of the people or groups concerned accept a different point of view. Where feelings are involved (and when are they not involved?), the extent of change depends on the level of involvement and the interpersonal climate that can be achieved. Involvement at deep enough levels for significant changes in attitudes and learning to take place is possible only in an open and supportive psychological atmosphere where defensive reactions are minimized and interpersonal empathy and support are maximized.

Each of these processes, then, is related to the others. Purposeful communication cannot take place when those involved are uncooperative. By uncooperative we mean unwilling to find a mutually acceptable basis for understanding or unable to set aside antagonistic points of view. At the same time, a knowledge of what human communication is and how it affects a relationship can help to alleviate conflict. It may even point the way toward better collaboration. Change, likewise, can be both a product of and a contributory variable in the improvement of communication and cooperation. A change in attitude toward another, for example, can result from sharing a satisfying experience such as a conversation where empathy exists on both parts.

A SET OF PROPOSITIONS ON INTERPERSONAL RELATIONS IN ORGANIZATIONS

In the following chapters we shall explore certain propositions which are related to the foregoing discussion. They are

1. *There are untapped resources of human cooperation in the organizational society.*

2. *Human cooperation is based on an optimistic view of the nature of man.*

3. *Whether we are optimistic or pessimistic about a man's basic nature is a function of our own needs and motives, which are learned, and not a function of inherited qualities in others.*

4. *Knowledge of self is therefore the key to human potentialities in inter-personal relations; it is learning and accepting what we are.*

5. *Learning and accepting what we are requires, with the help of others, a critical examination of our self-concept under conditions which permit a new evaluation of those elements of past experience which may be "defensing out" a part of the present.*

6. *Learning processes which build upon our internal capacities and abilities rather than those which inject external remedies are more effective for this purpose.*

7. *As a carrier of values essential to organizational survival, a manager or leader must be sensitive to his own personal characteristics and assumptions and to his impact on the growth and development of other individuals within the organization.*

8. *This sensitivity to himself and others involves a high degree of competence in such basic interpersonal processes as cooperation, communication, and change.*

In our explorations of these propositions, we have made a number of assumptions with which the reader may or may not find himself in agreement. Many of them are simply a matter of the values we hold and are perhaps not amenable to scientific scrutiny at this time. Others have some scientific basis which we have not documented, although we cannot say with certainty that any of them are Truth spelled with a capital T. Some may seem obvious to the point of naïveté, others may seem inconsistent, and still others obscure, but we list them without apology in the belief that there is some food for thought in all of them and that some will be worthy of research whenever science provides suitable tools. Here they are:

1. *Man has the capacity to be good rather than evil.*

2. *The organization is an instrument of man rather than the other way around.*

3. *Modern organizations seem pessimistic rather than optimistic concerning the nature of man.*

4. *Cooperation is a more natural state of human relations than competition.*

5. *The Existential Ethic is more appropriate to today's society than the Protestant Ethic.*

6. *In today's organizational society, democratic methods and values are nearly always preferable to autocratic.*

7. *Open organizations are more capable of growing and developing than closed ones.*

8. *Openness in interpersonal relations leads to personal growth and development and to more effective interpersonal communication; it facilitates essential change processes.*

9. *The human personality is not fixed. Under proper conditions, it can be changed in significant ways.*

10. *Building* on *man's capacities is better than building* in *remedies.*

11. *Self is a combination of personal initiative and conformity; man is both pilot and robot.*

12. *The self-concept is a primary motivator of human behavior.*

13. *Leadership is more than leading; it is also a helping relationship.*

14. *Man is more an end than means, i.e., he has potential which is prior to and superior to his uses as an instrument.*

CHAPTER TWO

NATURE OF MAN: PESSIMISTIC VIEW[1]

"We all know how little boys love fighting. They get their heads punched. But they have the satisfaction of having punched the other fellow's head."

HENRI BERGSON

One of the first problems we must deal with in human relationships concerns the primary assumptions we make about the nature of other people. Is the man we encounter in our daily lives good, evil, or something in between? What difference does it make? In this and the following chapter we shall explore these questions, looking first at some pessimistic and then at some optimistic views of human nature, and seeing how these views have influenced social thought.

The point is constantly made that traditional organizations work on the assumption that people are essentially opposed to work and lack the capacity for self-direction and personal responsibility. Modern theories of organization take the opposite view, i.e., people do have the capacity to become psychologically involved in cooperative activity and, under certain conditions, to be virtually self-motivated and self-controlled.

Douglas McGregor, among others, has noted how these implicit assumptions about the nature of man influence organization and leadership in his now classic discussion of Theory X and Theory Y. The former assumes that man is innately lazy and unreliable, and leads to organization and control based on external or imposed authority. The latter assumes that man can be basically self-directed and creative at work if properly motivated; this assumption is said to lead toward an integrative organizational strategy.

---

[1]   This chapter is adapted from "Human Relations and the Nature of Man" by Henry P. Knowles and Borje O. Saxberg, *Harvard Business Review*, March–April, 1967.

However, neither McGregor nor other writers in this field have undertaken to reveal how deeply the roots of these assumptions about man penetrate our culture and thus how powerfully they influence human relations in our society. Not only are these assumptions important in theories of human organization, but they are also crucial in every system of thought involved with human and social control. Whether concerned with organizational strategy, the ancient social order of the Zuni, or the political theories of a Machiavelli or a Locke, one cannot escape the underlying relatedness and importance of what is assumed about man himself.

Managers need to know more about the nature, sources, and effects of each of these assumptions in order (1) to sort out and understand their own ideas about the nature of humanity, and (2) to evaluate the fundamental influence of these ideas on managerial decisions. No other variable weighs more heavily on the ultimate form and quality of organizational and interpersonal relations.

The question of the basic nature of man is, of course, as old as history and probably as old as society itself. The argument, in its many forms, stems from the ancient philosophical debate as to whether man is an end or a means. Reducing the argument to its simplest terms, and considering only the extremities of the spectrum, we treat a person as an end when we permit him to establish his own purposes and to choose and decide for himself. Contrariwise, we treat a person as a means when we assume that he will cooperate only when forced to do so, when we limit his choices, and utilize him primarily as an instrument for our own ends and purposes.

Implicit in these ideas are central assumptions concerning (a) whether man is "good" or "evil," (b) whether he has the ability to cooperate voluntarily or must be forced to cooperate, (c) whether he is a "pilot" capable of choosing or a "robot" imprisoned by circumstances and incapable of choice. Ideas such as these lie at the very core of philosophies of religion, politics, education, organization, and human relations.

The choice of one or the other of these sets of assumptions has influenced a number of systems of thought concerned with questions of human regulation and control. We do not intend to emphasize the growing body of empirical evidence which indicates that the quality of individual and group performance varies from one kind of assumption and system to the other. This area is adequately covered in the writings of such men as Chris Argyris, Rensis Likert, Victor Vroom, and Douglas McGregor. Rather, we shall explore some of the cultural roots and branches of optimistic-pessimistic assumptions about human nature in order to show that an underlying unity exists along this dimension in a variety of human-social control systems.

Attitudes about human nature range from pessimism to optimism—from assigning to it evilness, predatory competition, and aggression on the one hand, to goodness, cooperation, and virtue on the other. Between these polar aspects we find the central predispositions of men and, therefore, of the social order. Let us begin our discussion by examining how certain ideas about human-social control have been affected by the pessimistic or "means" view of man. This is the attitude that man is essentially evil and driven by aggressive and uncooperative motives and drives.

FEAR VERSUS LOVE

As early giants in the history of Western idea makers, Niccolo Machiavelli and Thomas Hobbes—a pair of political scientists—provide us with a suitable starting point. It will be recalled that Machiavelli, in *The Prince* (1515), urged that, because of man's rebellious and uncooperative behavior, he must be strictly and ruthlessly controlled by anyone who aspires to gain or maintain a position of power. A ruler, in his view, must put aside any question of morality and must achieve control at any price and by whatever means he can find:

"It is much safer to be feared than loved . . . For it may be said of men in general that they are ungrateful, voluble, dissemblers, anxious to avoid dangers, and covetous of gain."

In all fairness, however, it must be made clear that he did not advocate his "end justifies the means" philosophy to benefit the prince or the ruler but to benefit the people. He assumed that only the ruler is competent to judge what the necessary ends are and must be. In furtherance of these ends, then, the ruler must resort to means which appear ruthless and deceitful.

Hobbes in *The Leviathan* (1651) outlined a theory of social relationships which makes him a direct intellectual descendant of Machiavelli. According to Hobbes, since men covet prestige, material goods, and power, and expect to attain these at their discretion, they live in perpetual fear of their neighbors:

"And therefore if any two men desire the same thing, which nevertheless they cannot both enjoy, they become enemies."

Law must therefore define what is honest and virtuous. But, in order for law to be applicable, a common authority must exist to enforce it. Man recognizes this need out of fear of loss of life and property. As a consequence, he enters into a social contract in which he gives up to a central authority certain rights he has had in nature. In this way, he brings about the creation of a commonwealth ruled by a sovereign. Each man is individually bound to this authority or Leviathan, and the latter's powers are irrevocable. The sovereign is a despot; whatever he wills becomes the people's will. As the Leviathan, he represents the supremacy of law, absolute authority and power, and the bureaucracy of the state.

SURVIVAL OF THE FITTEST

Both Machiavelli and Hobbes viewed human nature primarily as a product of experience. They perceived in mankind a predominance of aggressive and selfish motives as a result of socialization rather than biological inheritance, and they designed political systems in order to constrain and control human behavior and thus create order in society.

Orderliness in nature as a whole was evident to Charles Darwin. Through his research into the causes of variations in species and the contribution of these variations to the survival of species in nature, he became convinced that survival was assured through a process of natural selection. He thought that survival was guaranteed only to those who were the best representatives of the species and best adapted to the conditions of the environment. The survivors were those who through physical prowess and mental agility were able to win in the competition for food and mate. The suggestion here is clear, that nature is a never-ending struggle—a competition—and that a permanent state of war exists among and between all species and the natural environment.

Darwin's interpreters suggested that as with animals, so with man. Herbert Spencer, who was quick to find social implications in Darwin's biological theory, argued that among men the fittest survive; indeed, they are the only ones entitled to survive. Accordingly, the process of natural selection in man's world favors the aggressive and the strong. Man, in this scheme, is a predatory creature. Spencer's interpretations of Darwinian theory underlie much of the creed of many nineteenth century United States industrialists and their philosophy of the "stewardship" of the rich and the "gospel of wealth."

Darwin himself was not willing to accept Spencer's theory that the law of natural selection applied to the human race. Actually, he turned the argument around. Man's weakness, Darwin thought, becomes his greatest strength; it forces man to establish cooperative relationships with others for protection and maintenance. In addition, Darwin attributed to man a moral feeling—one of sympathy and compassion—rather than indifference toward the weak and defective. Unhappily, it has been his fate to become associated with "survival of the fittest" as a scientific theory applicable to man as well as to other natural species.

THE INVISIBLE HAND

Often associated with Darwin as a supporter of the idea of self-regulation in human society is Adam Smith. A century earlier, he placed his special emphasis on the automaticity of economic affairs. Under his doctrine of the invisible hand, there is just allocation of a nation's scarce resources through the price mechanism which reflects supply and demand in the market. By pursuing his self-interest, each individual can further not only his own fortune but also that of society as a whole.

It is this idea of self-interest as prime mover which has led many to assume that Smith considered man to possess basically a selfish rather than a virtuous nature. The economic doctrine of laissez-faire which Smith originated has meant "permission to do or make what you choose"; hence, non-interference with personal indulgence. This, when combined with self-interest as motivator, would seem, ergo, to support the notion that man is by nature self-seeking, predatory, and interested only in his own good at the expense of his weaker and less fortunate fellows. For example:

"It is not from the benevolence of the butcher, the brewer, or the baker that we expect our dinner, but from their regard of their own interest. We address ourselves not to their humanity, but to their self-love, and never talk to them of our own necessities, but of their advantage."

Although there is ample evidence to indicate that Smith, like Darwin, recognized that morality and government must and do govern the actions of men, he has nevertheless become, with Darwin, a symbol of individualism.

Smith at one time occupied a professorial chair in moral philosophy. In *The Theory of Moral Sentiment* (1759) he made it clear that he relied on natural law and, as a reflection of that, on a natural morality which prescribed three cardinal virtues: justice, prudence, and benevolence. Although he recognized some truth in the aphorism that private vices become public virtues, he clearly assumed that men in pursuit of enlightened self-interest are characterized by adherence to justice—"a scrupulous refusal ever to hurt or injure anyone else, in the pursuit of one's own interest or advantage." Smith was not concerned with production and the accumulation of goods per se, but rather with the ends served thereby. In effect, the welfare of the ordinary man was on his mind to such an extent that he implicitly took the side of the underdog, which he perceived the ordinary laboring man to be.

SEX AND AGGRESSION

Sigmund Freud, the father of psychoanalysis and the first to explore man's unconscious mind, took a clearer position on human nature than did Machiavelli, Hobbes, Darwin, or Smith. According to Freud, man is motivated by innate instincts and drives that he constantly struggles to pacify in ways which are antithetical to the laws of society. (These instincts and drives have been identified with sex and aggression but were really intended by Freud to refer to nature's and man's hankering to stay alive.) To the extent that society succeeds in curbing these animal forces, man becomes civilized and his energies can be turned toward socially acceptable goals. But, said Freud pessimistically:

"Psychoanalysis has concluded . . . that the primitive, savage, and evil impulses of mankind have not vanished in any individual, but continue their existence, although in repressed state . . . and . . . they wait for opportunities to display their activity."

Freud further observed, in his *Civilization and Its Discontents* (1930), that society, itself, is perpetually threatened by the underlying hostilities which exist between human beings. Periodically, these feelings explode into open aggression which persists until the participants can once more be brought under control. However, society's attempts to neutralize destructive impulses through a "cultural superego," which defines for man what is "good" and what is "bad," create feelings of guilt. This, Freud said, creates man's most urgent and important problem. The anxieties generated by this constant clash between man's basic nature and the demands and needs of society increase human unhappiness and can lead to mental illness. Thus, Freud seems to suggest, man is essentially doomed:

"From his (Freud's) point of view society, by its very nature, forces man to repress his inborn aggression more and more. The outlook for the future is that the more civilized he becomes, the more potentially destructive he becomes."

WARRIOR AND WEAPONMAKER

Recent evidence has been uncovered which seems to support the idea that man has been an aggressor and warrior since the beginning of his existence. Under the direction of L. S. B. Leakey, excavations conducted in South Africa— among what now appear to be the earliest remnants of man's ancestors—have uncovered man's earliest tools and have established that among them weapons occupied the most important place. The indications are that these were used not only for killing in the acqustion of food but also against man—for protection, in the defense of mate or of territory, and in the conduct of war. While the evidence is mixed, it has led some to theorize that a warlike, aggressive nature is a part of every man's inheritance.

As a consequence, it can be argued that Darwin's law of nature, survival of the fittest, also applied to man. Such an emphasis on aggression over a span of hundreds of thousands of years, Robert Ardrey has argued, must have had a permanent effect on his hereditary structure:

"Man is a predator with an instinct to kill and a genetic cultural affinity for the weapon."

In this view the urge to aggression, the desire to dominate others, is an instinct or drive transmitted from generation to generation through the genes.

The predisposition of men toward aggression has also been noted by one of the most renowned philosophers of our own time, Henri Bergson, who wrote:

"But no matter the thing taken, the motive adduced: the origin of war is ownership, individual or collective, and since humanity is predestined to owner- ship by its structure, war is natural. So strong, indeed, is the war instinct, that it is the first to appear when we scratch below the surface of civilization in search of nature. We all know how little boys love fighting. They get their heads punched. But they have the satisfaction of having punched the other fellow's head."

Bergson clearly joins with those who take a pessimistic view of man. By assuming that innate, predatory, and selfish instincts are first causes, he cannot conceive of a human society—with its dependence on material possessions—as capable of avoiding conflict through the processes of reason and self-control.

MANAGER AND MANAGED

The underlying ideas about human nature which have been previously outlined will also be found among those thinkers whose work focuses on the relationship between the manager and the managed in business and industry. Among them are the writers who are generally associated with the scientific management movement and who date from about 1900.

At this time, Fredrick W. Taylor, already mentioned, who pioneered this movement in the United States, saw a need for management to exert close control over the indifferent behavior of workmen in order to ensure their adherence to the objectives and goals of business enterprise. In spite of all the human values which have been imputed to his writings, it seems clear that Taylor and his followers made these six basic assumptions about human nature:

1. The employee is a "constant" in the production equation. The implication here is that man has a fixed nature.
2. The employee is an inert adjunct of the machine, prone to inefficiency and waste unless properly programmed.
3. The employee is by nature lazy; only managers honor the "hard work" creed of the Protestant Ethic.
4. The employee's main concern is self-interest. At work, this is always expressed in economic values.
5. Given appropriate expression, these values make man fiercely competitive among his peers as an accumulator of financial rewards.
6. Man (at least the working man) must therefore be tightly controlled and externally motivated in order to overcome his natural desire to avoid work unless the material gains available to him are worth his effort.

In accordance with these assumptions, Taylor thought that management must assume the responsibility for specifying in detail the *method* to be followed by the employee in order to gain an approximation of his full output potential. In addition, a *piece-rate plan* would have to be included as a financial incentive to ensure maximum performance.

At about the same time, Max Weber, a contemporary of Taylor's, was developing a similar pattern of thought in Europe regarding the relationship between manager and managed. While Taylor concerned himself mainly with the shop environment, Max Weber designed the features of his ideal bureaucracy viewing the organization from the top downward. In the elements of Weber's bureaucracy—specialization of personnel, impersonality, a hierarchy of authority relationships, entry and advancement by competitive examination, written policies, rules and procedures, and others—we find the Weberian image of man as a reluctant cog in an organizational machine. Thus the great majority of employees are confined to tightly controlled and dependent relationships with their superiors.

The pervasiveness of the Taylor-Weber approach to organization and management is evident throughout industrial organization today. Management scholars, such as Urwick, Mooney, and Brown, as well as important business executives like Cordiner of General Electric, Greenwalt of DuPont, and Kappel of AT&T, have generally adhered to this model of managerial control and the underlying values which emphasize the need to minimize employee resistance to work, and the consequent need for autocratic rule and a traditional bureaucratic hierarchy.

SUMMARY

Summarizing briefly the preceding discussion of the impact of a pessimistic view of human nature on social control, these common threads would seem to emerge:

1. Man is good in a state of nature but is transformed by the nature of society into a predator and power-seeker; or
2. Man is by nature evil, i.e., he is born with certain instincts or drives which lead him to war on other men. As a result of these conditions,
3. Man cannot be trusted to exercise self-control, but must be treated as a means or instrument and constrained if society is to survive.

This constraint or control over his actions may be accomplished by instilling in him fear of the ruler or leader. His behavior may be controlled by covenant, that is, through mutual adherence to the provisions of a "social contract" or an "employment contract" in which, in order to save himself, man gives up his natural rights to a "Leviathan" or superior whose power is absolute. Control may be accomplished through the automatic self-adjustment of natural selection or competition—the immutable law of biological inheritance or the "invisible hand" of the market-place—or it may be established through the power of lethal weapons to conquer and destroy. Finally, it may be effected through an organizational design which tends to emphasize man's weakness and need for guidance and direction. In all these cases, the view is pessimistic, the sources of constraint are external, extrinsic, detached, and objective. Man is a brute whose potential for resistance, opposition, aggression, and destruction require that he be rigidly controlled by impersonal forces wielded by those who have a power advantage or by restraints which function automatically within a given system.

CHAPTER THREE

NATURE OF MAN:
MAN AS A CREATIVE, SOCIAL BEING[1]

"The principle of cooperation is the most dominant and biologically the most important."

ASHLEY MONTAGU

Now let us turn from the foregoing cynical view of the nature of man to the view which emphasizes man's strength as a potentially creative, social being. As in dealing with the opposite view discussed earlier, we shall examine how an assumption that human beings have worth and goodness influences a wide-ranging sample of systems of social control. The examples used are not intended to be other than illustrative, straddling such divergent systems of human thought as political government, psychoanalysis, sociology, and business organization.

SOCIAL INSTINCT AND REASON

Although separated in time by sixteen centuries, Marcus Tullius Cicero and John Locke shared remarkably similar ideas about the governing of men. Cicero in *On the Commonwealth* (51 B.C.) argued that men by nature believe in goodness and well-doing, and abhor savagery and baseness. On the assumption of mutual advantage, they come together in obedience to a social instinct, and, where enough individuals are involved, form a democratic association or common-

---

[1]   Knowles and Saxberg, *op. cit.*

wealth for the benefit of all. Out of this emerges a leader who governs voluntary subjects through a moral claim to their allegiance rather than through regulation based on force.

Locke, in *The Second Treatise of Government* (1690) contended that men of reason are inherently disposed toward mutual support and cooperation:

"The state of nature has a law of nature to govern it, which obliges everyone; and reason, which is that law, teaches all mankind who will but consult it that, being all equal and independent, no one ought to harm another in his life, health, liberty, or possessions."

In other words, Locke argued that man's fundamental potential is reason and *reason itself* establishes cooperation as the basis for human relationships.

Under Locke's concept of the social contract, agreement is reached between free men to entrust to the community the authority to protect the common welfare. This custodianship is continued through tacit consent and is subject to the rule of the majority. For Locke, man is naturally disposed toward doing good, and government is essentially a convenience. The sovereign is assumed to will what the people will. Locke believed that man's mind at birth is a *tabula rasa*, a blank sheet of paper and, therefore, that man becomes a person through sense impressions, mediated by reason, which he derives from social experience.

Thus the human mind and character are shaped by interaction with the world; whatever man becomes is a function of reason and social interaction. The function of government, therefore, is not to create its own laws as a controlling force but to discover what natural forces bring man to a state of reason *in which he can control himself.*

COOPERATION AND SURVIVAL

Two men of science, W. C. Allee, a biologist, and Ashley Montagu, a cultural anthropologist, have advanced ideas from their own fields about human nature which correspond in important respects with those of Cicero and Locke. They have argued that nature, from a biological standpoint, supports the concept of survival through cooperation rather then competition.

Allee reported in his *Cooperation Among Animals* the results of a wealth of research which provide evidence that cooperative, social relationships increase the probability of survival for any single individual as well as for a species as a whole. One of his simple experiments showed that it takes a solution of proportionately less toxic colloidal silver to kill a single goldfish in an aquarium than it does to kill a number of goldfish. He suggested that the ability of a group of goldfish to neutralize a poison appears to increase faster than that of a single goldfish. He concluded his discussion of complex animal life in this way:

"The conclusion seems inescapable that the more closely knit societies arose from some sort of simple aggregation . . . such an evolution could come about most readily with the existence of an underlying pervasive element of unconscious proto-cooperation, or automatic tendency toward mutual aid among animals."

As Allee explored further evidence of cooperation in higher animals, he came to this conclusion:

"All through the animal kingdom—from amoeba to insects, or to man— animals show automatic unconscious proto-cooperation or even true cooperation. There is much evidence that the drift toward natural cooperation is somewhat stronger than the opposing tendency toward disoperation ⌊*among crowded animals*⌋*."*

However, in spite of his argument that a cooperative-social instinct is readily found in nature, Allee also recognized a counter-principle. This principle was that threat or force will be employed on the part of individuals, animal or man, to dominate others in a group in order to establish a hierarchy or pecking order. And he felt impelled to add that "Much can be said for an established order of dominance and subordination."

Allee pointed to evidences from the animal world which seem to reveal that any single individual thrives better where the pecking order is firmly established than where constant reorganization is in progress. He also saw evidence for this on the world scene. However, in all cases, Allee believed there will finally appear a subordinate to challenge the existing order. Thus, he concluded that a pecking order brings peace and stability for the *short* run, but that an integrated unit characterized by natural cooperation promises stability for the *long* run.

Montagu agreed in all essential respects with Allee. He argued that from a biological point of view men prefer to survive through cooperation rather than competition:

"The principle of cooperation is the most dominant and biologically the most important."

Montagu, of course, was concerned with man rather than with the animal world in general. He believed that man from infancy on must rely on others for the satisfaction of his needs, and therefore that affinity for interdependence is a fundamental reflection of the social state:

"All of man's natural inclinations are toward the development of goodness, toward the continuance of states of goodness and the discontinuance of unpleasant states."

Thus warfare is considered by Montagu, as it was by Allee, as a human invention derived from economic or materialistic, rather than biological considerations.

"BLANK PAGE" CONCEPT

On the basis of their more sanguine views of man's nature, these men, from Cicero through Montagu, have set forth behavioral concepts which support the idea that cooperation outweighs aggression in human relationships, and that these relationships can be strengthened through a constructive process of learning. Much of modern thought in psychoanalysis and psychotherapy, in sociology and social psychology, and in the field of organizational studies is also based on an optimistic view of man's nature. It resists Descartes' assumption that men are born with innate ideas and a more or less given nature.

Thus many modern behavioral scientists tend, like Locke, to think of man as entering life with a mind like a blank page on which experience is then impressed, molding the form and content of his personality. According to this way of thought, man's behavior is acquired as a result of experience in life, and it changes with experience. It is not solely predetermined by the genes, nor is it fixed and irrevocable. Out of these views have emerged new ways of perceiving man as an individual and as a member of a group.

Earlier, we outlined the pessimistic view of man on which Freud based his psychoanalytic theory. Freud's assumption about man's innate nature affected his theories in the same way as Hobbes' assumptions about man influenced his theories of government and society: Man, left to his own devices, will prey on other men to satisfy his desires and must, in the interests of all, be restrained by forces in society.

The psychoanalysts who followed Freud have made distinctive contributions to modern views of the nature of man. From among them has emerged a group which broke with Freud on the issue of the basic nature of man, the so-called neo-Freudians, represented in this discussion by Harry Stack Sullivan, Erich Fromm, and Karen Horney. The neo-Freudians base their theories of human behavior on the assumption that the development of personality is influenced primarily by external societal forces and events rather than by biogenetically determined, innate instincts or drives.

Freud, of course, assumed that man and society are basically divided— on the one hand, a set of drives in man (sex and aggression) which are at the root of man's evil and, on the other, a set of rules derived from man's needs in the human culture which inhibit and control the individual. The neo-Freudians argue that there is no dichotomy between man and society. According to Fromm:

"The most beautiful as well as the most ugly inclinations of man are not a part of a fixed and biologically given human nature but result from the social process."

Necessarily then, if man is to be understood, major attention must be given to those forces in his environment which influence the molding of his personality.

J. A. C. Brown in *The Social Psychology of Industry* has described the difference between Freudian and neo-Freudian ideas about the nature of man as being "pushed from behind" or "drawn from in front." This, in a rough way, is the difference between

psychological determinism or behaviorist psychology with its focus on drives, instincts, or the conditioned reflex as a source of behavior and

subjectivist theories of psychology which perceive psychic energy as being derived from personal goals and personal perceptions of reality.

Sullivan's theory of personality development, like Fromm's and Horney's, belongs in this latter category.

According to Sullivan, the individual begins life with certain potentials and two basic goals: satisfaction and security. The extent to which he realizes his potential and achieves his goals depends on his experiences with other people. The pursuit of "satisfaction" has to do with satisfying physical needs like sleep, hunger, and sex.

However, the manner in which such needs are satisfied does not depend on the innate characteristics of an individual but reflects behavior patterns which are the product of interpersonal relations. It is in relation to other people that an individual seeks "security"—that is, in the avoidance of anxiety caused by feelings of disapproval or inadequacy in a social situation. Thus the matter of psychological security is culture-bound, and the form and content of the human personality is a product of specific cultural forces.

Sullivan defines the anxiety-free condition of "euphoria" as a tensionless state similar to that experienced by a new-born and sleeping child who has yet to discover that he has arrived in a threatening environment. Such an infant is at peace with the world, or, in Rousseau's terms, in a state of oneness and harmony with nature. Only exposure to the anxieties which arise out of human relationships can change this profound sense of well-being into a state of tension. This state of tension then promotes education and learning through which the self-system of an individual finally emerges.

The *self-system*, as Sullivan defines it, represents that portion of an individual's potential which is realized, while the *true self* contains the maximum potentialities which could have been developed under ideal conditions of experience. Since it is an unfortunate fact of life in our culture that interpersonal experience is far from ideal, Sullivan felt that most people are "inferior caricatures of what they might have been."

CULTURAL DETERMINATION

Fromm does not accept the "blank page" concept of Locke but, nevertheless, strongly rejects the idea that instincts are the primary source of human behavior. Fromm concedes that man comes into existence with a set of drives and instincts. However, he argues that their particular patterns of development and their manifestation in the behavior of individuals are culturally determined:

"Any given social order does not create these fundamental strivings but it determines which of the limited number of potential passions are to become manifest or dominant."

From this, it is clear that Fromm considers that human potentialities depend to a very large extent on the *will to productiveness which society succeeds in bringing to man*. The individual is shaped by society. The environment in which the individual exists, therefore, becomes a primary factor in the way he responds to life and work.

Fromm emphasizes in his theory that man is faced with a desire to be part of nature. Animals, through their instinctual equipment, seem able to accommodate themselves to the external environment through what appears to be an automatic process and, therefore, to achieve close ties with nature. Man, in contrast, through self-awareness and reason is alienated from nature.

In fact, in industrial society he is often alienated from himself, from meaningful human relationships, and from his work. In this process man is caught in a tug-of-war between self-reliance, power, control over nature, independence, and escape from isolation, competition, hostility, and insecurity. He must find his path by relating to things and to people. Ideally, he should succeed in establishing a productive relationship in which he is able to feel and act in accordance with his potential for contributing to constructive human life.

PILOT OR ROBOT?

As our final example of modern psychoanalytic thought, we consider Karen Horney. In her writings Horney agrees with Sullivan and Fromm in the view that Freud gave biological and genetic factors an excessive role in character formation. Taking the position that man's nature is not instinctive but learned, she was one of the first analysts to emphasize the importance of interpersonal relations in behavior development. What an individual learns—that is, how he reacts to life with others—is influenced most by the way be is treated by others.

It was Horney's view that all individuals in their natural development seek sentiments of liking and approval from others. Where interpersonal relationships do not have such support, anxiety develops and begins to interfere with the growth of a healthy personality. In such cases people respond to others in three basic ways: (1) by "moving toward people"—feeling inadequate, they become attached and dependent; (2) by "moving against people"—rejected, they become rebellious and aggressive; or (3) by "moving away from people"— they seek comfort for rejection in symbolic substitutes and fantasy. Neurotic behavior occurs when there is conflict over which response pattern to adopt in a given situation. Various defense mechanisms help solve such conflicts but at the expense of genuineness in human relationships and of needed problem-solving behavior.

Because of her emphasis on the importance of situational factors in personality development, Horney tended to look to a person's present interpersonal involvements for the causes and solutions to neurotic problems. She did not deny that a connection existed between an individual's current responses and his early life—a connection which was so important a part of Freud's thinking—but she argued that one must look to the present situation for clues as to what triggered these responses.

Man is not, therefore, doomed by a set of prenatally determined instincts, nor are his patterns of behavior irrevocably established by early life experience. Horney's concept of man is cheerful and optimistic, not gloomy and pessimistic. Man is born neither a devil nor a saint; he simply reflects in his behavior the nature of relationships developed since the time of his birth with people who have been important to him.

These insights into human nature which summarize the thinking of an important school of modern psychotherapy are based on the confident viewpoint that man is not doomed by a fixed and evil nature from which he cannot escape. Rather, they would seem to suggest just the opposite: man has within himself the potential to grow and develop significantly in cooperation with others. Man is a pilot, not a robot. What is needed is a means of tapping man's potential for joining in productive relationships with others.

INDIVIDUAL OR ENVIRONMENT?

One of the first social scientists to apply this concept of man to analysis of industrial organizations was Elton Mayo of Harvard University, the Director during the 1930's of the extensive research program at the Hawthorne Plant of the Western Electric Company. Mayo's view of human nature was optimistic and anti-Freudian. To illustrate:

"The concealed assumption of the doctrine of original sin invalidates the psychoanalytic findings. The theory that life is a strenuous fight to subdue perversion, that the human mind is by nature "pathogenic" (i.e., predisposed to the pathological) is not a starting point for biological observation."

In other words, the concept that life on earth is an atonement for original transgressions of God's laws, and that man is cursed with a set of evil instincts which must be curbed by society, is inadequate as a base for observing and understanding man's behavior in daily life.

Mayo argued that too much attention was being given in industrial settings to *individuals* as the source of noncooperative and unproductive relationships between the leaders and the workers in an organization. He pointed out that developments in sociology and in social anthropology had already opened to serious question whether a merely psychological study of individuals in an organization is a logical approach to a comprehension of their behavior as workers.

On the contrary, Mayo said, such individuals constitute a group which develops responses to the total organizational environment. The research program which he headed at the Hawthorne Plant appeared to provide him with convincing evidence. Consequently, the interview program, originally consisting of isolated interviews, was restructured so that interviewers were assigned to study individuals over extended periods of time in relation to their jobs, the informal social organization in which they worked, and company policy.

The original isolated interviewing method was based on the premise that personal behavior or misbehavior was a result of personal rationality or irrationality; the second method was based on the assumption that the individual was only one of a number of interdependent variables relating to behavior. These other variables were part of the working environment and included such factors as leadership, working conditions, and working group membership. Science, inspired by the work of early sociologists and anthropologists, was at last beginning to show, contrary to Hobbesian theory, that man was more victim than antagonist in his environment.

BEHAVIORAL SCIENCE MAN

While the initial thrust toward change in managerial philosophy and practice can be traced back to the origin of the human relations movement in the 1930's, it has continued through the present time in two somewhat divergent directions: (1) toward the fusion of the scientific organizational behavior approach with a new, more humanistic management philosophy, and (2) toward organizational reeducation and change through sensitivity or laboratory training. In both cases the importance of the roles played by behavioral and other social scientists in defining the relationship between the manager and the managed is becoming more and more evident.

While Mayo's work resulted in increasing the emphasis on human relations mainly in normative terms, much of the subsequent direction of this work is based on the research and findings of the behavioral sciences of psychology and cultural anthropology. Research workers such as Argyris, McGregor, and Likert have identified themselves with A. H. Maslow's theory of the need hierarchy as an aspect of human nature. Given the assumption that a satisfied need does not motivate, man is seen as satisfying in ascending order the needs of hunger in an extended sense, safety, social affection, esteem, and finally self-actualization or self-fulfillment. In fact, Maslow now believes that this list must be further extended to include meta-self fulfillment which corresponds to a person's living up to a spiritual challenge which transcends himself.

The challenge for management today is seen by these authors as one of providing man at work with the opportunity to grow and mature continually into a human being who, because of a favorable working climate, is able to realize his own goals best by working for the success of the organization of which he is a member. Implicit in their assumptions is the idea that man has an essential nature which is defined by the broad spectrum of his needs, capacities, and tendencies. These needs, as expressed by Maslow, "are on their face good or neutral rather than evil."

In a continuing reflection of the neo-Freudian view of man, we find McGregor stating, "If employees are lazy, indifferent, unwilling to take responsibility, intransigent, uncreative, uncooperative," their attitude is due to the traditional bureaucratic assumptions and methods of organization and control. Argyris, in a similar vein suggests, "Mutual understanding, trust, self-esteem, openness, internal commitment, fully functioning human beings who aspire to excellence ... these values can not only be protected, but indeed increased, in an industrial setting."

In the world of work, therefore, man is seen by the behavioral scientists as responding to the influences of his organizational environment. Given the opportunity, he participates creatively in furthering the objectives of the organization. If frustrated, his behavior characteristically reverts to aggression or he turns apathetic and slovenly, and becomes alienated from an orientation toward work as a central life interest.

Such a basic underlying belief in man as a creative human being oriented toward constructive rather than destructive activities is even more clearly represented in the sensitivity training movement. Through this process of re-education and skill development, Warren G. Bennis and his collaborators see the way to democratization of management—a condition which they view as essential in the face of accelerating technological change, the increasing proportion of professionals in the work force, and the consequent necessity of the organization to accept the values of science and scientific inquiry in order to survive in the future.

Democracy is here defined not as permissiveness or laissez faire but as a system of values by which people in organizations are assumed to feel "internally compelled" to live. These include free communication, the consensus principle, influence based on competence rather than position, acceptance of emotion as fact, and a "basically human bias" in dealing with conflict.

In Bennis' terms, the "organization man" becomes a signpost on the road pointing the way to the kinds of flexibility and adaptability which are essential if the democratic environment in which science and scientists can flourish is to be realized. Whether one agrees or not, it is well known among men of science that personalities are only of passing interest compared to the contribution they hope to make to the accumulation of new knowledge.

In the foregoing discussions two aspects of the questions of human nature and its impact upon social relationships have emerged. The first has to do with inner qualities people possess, the second with the training or socializing process. What Cicero called the social instinct, Locke has called reason. Both lead men to make assumptions about one another which provide the matrix for mutual cooperation and which reject the notion of predatory competition on the one hand, or indifference on the other, as the governing mode of human existence. Men come together in obedience to a social instinct based on an assumption of mutual advantage. An ethical system develops out of common consent and provides a moral or internal means of control in contrast to the brute force methods of the Hobbesian state. Reason distinguishes men from the animals, and reason rejects aggression as a basis for human relationships. Allee brings out the idea of survival as a motivating force. Biology, in Allee's view, provides evidence that active cooperation is the key to the preservation of a species, including man, a view which finds no support among the interpreters of Darwin but a view to which Montagu gives added weight from his studies in anthropology. The modern "man of behavioral science" finds the energy for his behavior within himself, but its quality is the product of inner force in interaction with environment. Men's choices are a result of need (energy) interpretations in relation to the way in which men perceive or evaluate their opportunities for need satisfaction in the environment. If suitable opportunities are absent, men become frustrated and reactive. In this view the "evilness" of men is born in man's frustrations and is not an inherent characteristic of human nature.

THE CONCEPT OF PRIMARY TENDENCY

We have here been concerned with how the evaluation of the quality of human nature affects the choice of ways to control man, particularly in situations where he can achieve his objectives only by associating with others. We have on the one hand considered man in terms of his social responses to other men in a posture of goodness or cooperation and on the other in a posture of evilness, indifference, or competition. We have confined the discussion to these polar conditions for the sake of simplicity and clarity, although it is, of course, a matter of common observation that all the possible social processes are located along a continuum whose polar extremities are cooperation and competition.

Cooperation and competition, as opposite ends of a spectrum, are closely related to love and hate, friendship and enmity, harmony and discord, collaboration and opposition. They therefore may be used to describe a person's *basic* or *characteristic* propensity toward his fellow man. In terms of his attitudes toward others, every man will find himself at some point on this spectrum depending upon the particular situation in which he is involved. However, each man is drawn by the force of his own history and subjective processes toward some primary tendency, some central quality of being which determines the general pattern of his social behavior. Peripheral changes occur in this pattern to accommodate the demands of the various roles he plays, but there would seem to be a core pattern which represents his basic beliefs concerning the nature of man. Man is evil or man is good, depending upon the individual's experience of mankind.

The examples we have cited from the history of human thought illustrate this concept of the *primary tendency* in the kind of view one man takes of another. They clearly indicate also that cooperation and competition, or goodness and evilness as human characteristics are not discrete activities or qualities but exist in various mixtures in human nature. Hobbes' *primary tendency*, for example, was to view man as evil. Nevertheless, his idea of the "social contract" contains the implicit assumption of *cooperative* activity among men by which they give up their rights to a ruling Leviathan to gain protection from one another. Bergson said that war in a materialistic society is natural, but noted that collective ownership leads to cooperation within groups to protect members from outsiders. Even Freud, who comes closest to a concept of innately evil men straining against societal constraints to satisfy their needs, conceded that man may become "good" because of his dependency upon others; he will, in short, *cooperate* when he finds helping behavior in other men.

Among those whose primary tendency is to view man as good we find similar ambivalencies. Locke argued that reason evoked cooperation among men. However, he implied that the "social contract" exists between ruler and ruled to control man's acquired *competitive*, aggressive nature. The neo-Freudians held that man's goodness or evilness was a product of experience, i.e., competitive (hating) experiences lead to malfunctioning by societal standards but cooperative (loving) experiences lead to satisfaction and development.

The psychoanalytic assumptions and clinical findings of the neo-Freudians to the effect that man has basic worth and is capable of constructive psychic responses in an environment of understanding and encouragement have received scientific support among modern experimenters. Behavioral Science Man, whether the setting has been in the laboratory or in the field, e.g., in a business, educational, or government organization, is a "good" man whose potential for productive growth and self-actualization has too often been stunted by rulers or managers who assumed that he was "bad" and consequently must be manipulated like a puppet.

The quality of human relations in any organization, from the political state to business enterprise, reflects first of all its members' and particularly its leaders' fundamental attitudes toward others, their views of the essential character of humanity itself. It makes a great deal of difference in systems of social control whether those involved tend to view man, in general, as good or evil. If we assume that man is good, we can believe that misbehavior is a reactive response rather than a manifestation of character. This attitude leads to a search for causes in his experience rather than in his nature. If we are to find a cause for behavioral failure, we must look outside the offender rather than inside, and thus consider a whole new range of variable and contributory circumstances.

If, on the other hand, we assume that man, himself, is bad, *a priori*, then we assume that his behavior is caused by something in himself which we cannot alter directly. Our attention must then focus on using external curbs or controls to limit his freedom of choice and action. In thus limiting the extent of overt behavior, we exclude ourselves from insight into powerful internal motives or sources of control. Which of the underlying human values predominates, becomes manifest or visible in the way social relationships are structured, in the kinds of rewards and penalties that are used, in the character of the communication process which links people together, and in the other elements of social control which characterize a relationship or an organization.

CHAPTER FOUR

A ROBOT CONCEPT OF PERSONALITY

"With respect to the formation of individual personalities, culture operates as one of a series of factors which also includes the physiologically determined potentialities of the individual and his relations with other individuals."

RALPH LINTON

We discussed the effect of different assumptions about human nature on human relationships as though man could be dichotomized as either good or bad, co-operative or competitive, and we gave examples of how one assumption or the other can lead to widely different theories of social control. We also introduced the idea of the *primary tendency*, that is, a person's characteristic attitude set toward other persons, pointing out that this tendency is the product of an individual's subjective processes and past relationships with other significant persons in his life, beginning from the moment of birth. The key to an individual's interpersonal style or distinctive and characteristic manner of relating to and controlling other people is, therefore, to be found in his personality. If we are to understand human behavior and especially how human attitudes and human conduct affect and are affected by the interactions of people with one another, we must examine how personality is formed and how, in some cases, it may be changed.

HUMAN NATURE AND THE PERCEIVER

Our discussion of the primary tendency or set of attitudes that each of us has toward others suggests that the nature of man is not a "given," having an independent existence, but is the product of each individual's unique human experience. That is, in his generalized, predominant, and fundamental definition of his fellow man, each individual reflects in the deepest sense his own history. This means that human nature cannot be described in universal, fixed, and absolute terms but only in relation to a perceiving individual. Human nature has no essence, no substance, no reality except as it is distilled from the ideas and interpretations of the individual human observer.

Consider the relationship between three persons, Mr. Anderson, Mr. Briggs, and Mr. Corey. To Mr. Anderson, another person, Mr. Briggs is viewed with suspicion, reserve, or even hostility, because this is Mr. Anderson's primary tendency or characteristic way of relating to people. To Mr. Cory, however, this same person, Mr. Briggs, is assumed to be "good" or at the least neutral in character and, unless proved otherwise, worthy of trust and confidence. The difference here is not to be found in Mr. Brigg's person but in the learned system of needs and attitudes of Mr. Anderson and Mr. Corey. To the observer, Mr. Anderson, Mr. Briggs is "evil" because Mr. Anderson has "learned" that nearly everyone is hostile and that life is a constant struggle against men's perversity, selfishness, and deceit. Mr. Anderson may hide his feelings behind a mask and may even seem benevolent and solicitous as long as he feels he is in control. But the basic or *primary tendency* of Mr. Anderson is still there though hidden and, as we suggest, is a constant influence on his characteristic ways of relating to other people. In contrast, the second observer, Mr. Corey, perceives Mr. Briggs as essentially "good" because experiences in the course of his life path have taught him to preface his interpersonal relations with a feeling and a projection of trust in others and to look upon others as a source of help and strength. As a consequence, Mr. Corey is more apt to find his way along cooperative paths in social relationships.

There are, it would seem, more Mr. Andersons in our organizational society than there are Mr. Coreys. There is a basic inclination in the American culture to compete with others for power, prestige, and possession because we have learned that these things can provide us with feelings of security in our personal relationships with others. This pervasive struggle for power, material and non-material, which occurs at every level of society, leads us to regard our fellow man with suspicion, even hostility, lest he stand in our way on our road to success. The existence of this underlying and diffused emphasis on interpersonal hostility makes every man a potential competitor of every other man. We are driven by the fear that we shall fail and thus lose status, self-esteem, and the satisfaction of other important needs. This ethic, carried over into the twentieth century from frontier days, leaves us with a feeling of isolation and a compensatory craving for affection, a craving which our more aggressive tendencies largely block from fulfillment. Furthermore, these feelings of mutual distrust lead many of us to look to the other *individuals* in our lives, particularly those upon whom we must depend, as the real or potential source of our failures. We therefore search for a means of control with which we can make them more predictable and responsive to our needs and demands.

Concepts of the nature of man and of personality have implications with respect to the whole question of leadership and leadership training, and the skills associated with interpersonal and organizational effectiveness. In this and the next chapter we shall begin to sort out these implications by examining first the objective and then the subjective modes of the human personality. These discussions are designed to pave the way for a later analysis of the self as it relates to the individual's awareness and acceptance of himself, the nature and sources of his needs and motives, and his attitudes toward other people.

OBJECTIVE AND SUBJECTIVE VIEWS OF PERSONALITY

Our assumptions about human nature are a product of status and role experiences in the culture *plus* our own *unique imprint* upon these experiences. Status is a person's position in society. Age, sex, and occupation, for example, help to determine where we fit in the social structure in relation to other persons. The concept of social role refers to the set or cluster of expectations people have concerning how a person occupying a certain role ought to behave. These expectations include those of the person occupying the position. Our personal role perceptions and interpretations constitute our individual stamp or mark upon our actual role behavior. In a play, for example, the part of an actor is strictly prescribed to the extent of the written dialogue and action, but his actual performance of the role will reflect his own ideas concerning the character he is portraying and his manner of speaking and acting. A Gielgud *Hamlet* is not a Burton *Hamlet*, and it is not an Olivier *Hamlet*. Each interpretation carries the "unique imprint" of the actor. At the same time each Hamlet is recognizable to the audience, though with varying individual reactions, because, on the whole, it meets their general expectations for the role.

Our behavior and attitudes (including our ideals and values), therefore, reflect the influence of both external and internal forces. Inputs from the culture and from the social structure are acted upon by our "personality," and the resultant output is a composite pattern of learned behavior and personal expression. In more technical terms, human conduct is the product of mutual, interacting patterns of influence originating in role (culture), position or status (society), and self (personality).

Personality, like culture and society, is a phenomenon of great complexity. While some of its parts can be observed and measured, other parts seem beyond the reach of currently available methods of scientific inquiry. Its inner workings are sometimes thought of as taking place in a windowless container or "black box," where internal operations and activities are not available for direct observation. We can really only see certain inputs and outputs of this container or "black box," as illustrated in Fig. 1.

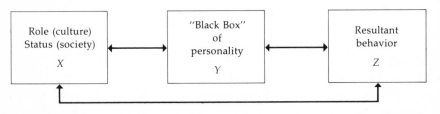

Fig. 1.   Personality-culture system.

This figure shows in schematic form the elements of the personality-society-culture system. Observable input from society and culture enters the "black box" of personality and the internal processes taking place are reflected in observable resultant behavior. This behavior, in turn, affects culture and society, thus closing the system.

In searching for an answer to the enigma of the human personality, writers seem to fall into one of two camps. Some emphasize phases X and Z, the external or outward manifestations of personality, focusing attention on social and cultural inputs and outputs and upon the *consequences* of interaction between the individual and his environment. According to them, what a person has learned from others explains his reactions to the experiences he encounters as he adapts to the world around him and, most importantly, to the people in it and to the social structures and rules of behavior by which they live. Other writers are more concerned with the *process* which takes place in the *mind*; they tend to look upon personality more as a reflection of the subjective-interactive operations which occur between a person's inner states of mind and the world of experience. These writers are mainly concerned with phase Y in Fig. 1, but they are also concerned with the interactive phases indicated by the double-ended arrows.

THE CULTURAL OR ROBOT CONCEPT OF PERSONALITY

One dimension of personality consists of inherited physiological components which include a genetically bounded range of potential individual development. However, according to those who emphasize that personality is a reflection of culture, beyond this organic base a socially derived pattern of personality emerges involving the particular experiences which a person has encountered. Initially he experiences them through intermediaries such as his parents, but later directly, as they become part of the learning process.

Thus, the newly born baby has certain innate capacities and potentialities buried in the chromosomes and genes which he inherited from an undeterminable past of family ancestors. This inheritance will be reflected in his facial features, in his physical outlines, and in his physiological and organic structures and processes. These likenesses give evidence of latent personality formation. They form the constitutional boundaries to what a person can become, but within these boundaries there exist, an infinite variety of possible personality patterns, any of which may become activated or remain neglected. In common experience, this heritage often is the basis for one of the first judgments made by society with reference to a new arrival when family and friends comment on his physical well-being, the character of his facial expressions, and his possible likeness to living relatives and parents.

Though an individual's starting point on life's arch may be placed before birth—and much evidence suggests that the period in the womb is one which is highly sensitive to environmental influences of nurture and emotions—we take as our starting point life as it begins at birth. That event in human society creates the necessity for preparedness on the part of society to receive and educate a new member.

This societal preparedness as well as all subsequent situations and events occurring during the individual's life span are largely culturally determined. All members of society act as depositories of knowledge, and their behavior reflects a process of learning as the experiences of older generations become available to them through written or oral tradition, or as contemporaries transmit to each other newly accumulated knowledge.

THE ASSIGNMENT OF STATUS

To each individual at birth every society assigns a status which will assure his being brought up in society's ways. In our culture, the status of the infant traditionally assures him of nurture from a mother within the family setting. The family unit represents a subculture which, in addition to adherence to the way of life approved by society in general, reflects unique features. These derive from the particular influences impinging on the family by virtue of acceptance of a particular religious faith or the absence of it, of the father's occupation, wealth, and position in society. The family's membership in a particular class in society is reflected in house and furniture, thoughts and beliefs, and goals and aspirations. This does not by any means exhaust the influences on a child stemming from familial life, but it does illustrate the multitude of influences which do not have a generalized cultural definition within society as a whole. There is, of course, a wide range of optional variations within different subcultures of society, and within any membership group in society.

AUTHORITY AND CONSCIENCE

In order for a child to grow up physically healthy we know it must have adequate nourishment and shelter. But we are much harder pressed to define the conditions under which a child will grow up mentally and psychologically healthy. Various societies have widely differing views as to what represents appropriate behavior for a child through the various stages of development. However, in every case and in every society he is supplied with a succession of teachers. In our society his education usually begins with the mother and father. Later his contacts extend to include other members of the family, friends in the neighborhood and in school, teachers in the various stages of educational pursuits and, in general, significant figures at all levels of learning from birth to death. Some have speculated that a child who is not able to bow to authority will not be able to learn, and therefore will prove unsuitable for socialization and development into a useful member of society. It is even suggested that *if personality is conceived to be a reflection of culture*, acceptance of authority must be an innate biological faculty built into the genes of man.

In line with the acceptance of authority is the concept of conscience. Man must develop very early in life a capacity for internalizing the values and norms of society in order to be able to behave in ways which society regards as normal, appropriate, and ethical. The development of a conscience appears to be inextricably tied to the child's learning to resist temptation. To instill this characteristic in a child, he must be taught to internalize the behavior approved in the society of which he is a member. In this process the child receives love and approval from those who have a position of importance in his world in exchange for his doing the right thing as they define it. After a brief period of self-indulgence, he discovers that life is not a bed of roses. While initially there seemed to be nothing that he could not have just by putting up a howl for it, at some point he suddenly becomes aware of a sinister undertone of deprivation. The child finds that he is expected to wait for his food until certain times, to lie quiet during the night, take a nap in the afternoon, use clothes which are sometimes uncomfortable, and generally put up with things which are more or less distasteful to him. Later this encroachment takes the form of more or less harsh demands—of toilet training, of behaving in company, of playing amicably with other children, and so on.

Some have speculated that a child learns appropriate behavior by identification with those whom he perceives to have resources which he regards as valuable and perhaps available as possible compensation to him. In other words, a child is taught to resist temptation by observing good behavior on the part of those he experiences as powerful or by observing which of his own behaviors they approve of as good. This line of reasoning leads to the conclusion that man belongs to the world of nature and, left alone, would be governed by instincts and drives which build up organic tensions requiring immediate gratification. Only society and civilization stand in the way, forcing man to act in learned ways to ensure that the survival of society and community takes precedence over individual needs.

Resistance to temptation becomes an easier process for the child as his internalized norms of behavior grow sufficiently strong to induce in him feelings of guilt. These feelings of guilt represent the manifest functioning of conscience. The latter imposes self-restraint from internal resources in contrast to the external controls imposed by adult mediators or supervisors.

Conscience or feelings of guilt do more than serve as a resistance or restraint upon temptation. On the positive side, introducing individuals to the accepted ways of society helps them to gain a set of values in terms of worthwhile objects or ends worthy of support and aspiration. In an extended sense, the positive aspect of conscience becomes the seat for a generalized ideal good, a concept frequently undergirding the belief system or religious faith which characterizes an individual's childhood and family background.

In more precise terms, we suggest that when personality is viewed as a product of cultural experience, each member of society is an incumbent of a status position from the moment of birth. As the infant grows and develops he becomes associated with other social groups where face-to-face relationships enable personal bonds of attachment to develop. In each of these social organizations, our individual also is assigned various status positions. In adolescence and adulthood he becomes associated with formal organizations where he will hold positions giving him authority over other members. It is important to recognize that these status positions have an existence over and beyond that of the position holder, who has only a limited time span in which to discharge the responsibilities placed upon him.

ROLE BEHAVIOR

The individual brings to his status position a certain set of innate abilities, as well as a set of experiences gained in an environment with certain characteristics. He will therefore enact a role which is a composite of his individuality and the requirements of the status position he occupies.

Other·persons in the environment perform the functions of role "senders" for the social system and its variety of status positions. Basing their projections on culturally perpetuated norms surrounding a status position, they communicate their role expectations to the position holder. He in turn experiences these pressures emanating from others as forces affecting his role behavior. These role pressures join the forces he brought with him into the position as a result of his prior internalization of values and norms. He must integrate these forces into a resultant behavior in performing his role. A person in his lifetime belongs to many social and formal organizations. At any moment in time he is likely to be an active member of a number of such organizations. Therefore, he represents a cluster of status positions and assumes roles he interprets as appropriate to them. The particular situation at any one time should determine which particular synthesis of position and role will provide him with standards of appropriate behavior.

The adult person may frequently develop a preference toward one particular position and role, however, and weigh his behavior in this direction regardless of the situation in which he finds himself. Similarly, a person may incorporate in his personality, role definitions which are incongruent and conflict with one another. He avoids being confronted with this conflict because the situations within which he operates never mix or overlap. He may cooperate, for example, in family projects, assuming a nondirective role, while being fiercely competitive and aggressive in his business life. He is able, in effect, to draw upon a compartmentalized set of standards.

A person may, moreover, be faced with *conflicting* role pressures in his association with different groups and organizations and in particular situations. These conflicts cannot be avoided, and will require his evaluation and decision. In such cases, the individual may be caught off guard and face role conflict and experience role strain when he finds that he cannot escape these diverse signals from role senders. Similarly, he may suffer internal role conflicts and role strain as he finds role forces confronting his personal value system and finds that he is unable to justify the behavior expected of him in a particular situation.

GROUP RELATIONSHIPS

These role conflicts and role strains experienced by the individual reflect an internalization of values and commitments to norms of groups which have been or are active reference groups for him. Groups which attract an individual's personal commitment to the group's values are *reference groups* to him. These may be the family, a social or professional group, or any other special group which has a strong attraction for the individual. Personality is influenced and molded mainly through the values and norms of reference groups. Even though a member with such a commitment to a group later leaves it, his personality will have been indelibly affected by affiliation with that group. We also observe that a person sometimes chooses as a reference group one of which he is not yet a member, or may never join as a member. He may aspire to membership in such a group and, through a process of anticipatory socialization, attempt to behave according to the standards he perceives for the group, hoping to receive approval and become acceptable for membership.

In contrast to his association with reference groups, an individual frequently is a member of other groups, pays membership fees, and is carried on the membership list. His membership in these groups is only perfunctory, however. It is also possible that a person may have membership in groups by ascription with no action on his part or even desire on his part to claim such membership. Consequently, reference groups are not necessarily membership groups, nor do membership groups necessarily become reference groups for an individual.

Since the organizational world is where man spends most of his waking hours, his personality also reflects the culture of the organization. The impact of the organizational group on the individual is transmitted through intermediaries. When an individual signs an employment contract, management expects that the signatory will conform to the requirements of the institution's objectives and goals. In addition, management assumes that the employee in so doing will conform to the underlying value system of the management.

The organization is inescapably confronted with work group members who influence it as a social culture with sentiments, emotions, feelings, and values reflecting personal objectives and goals which may or may not coincide with its own. Operational overlays develop as a product of the organizational subculture and become superimposed on the authority structure of the formal organization. These overlays in relationship to power, communication, friendship, work expertise, and other necessary functions assure for the organization a needed adaptation to the constantly changing environment. This emergent social system must include within its interest sphere not only the objectives and goals of the formal organization, but also the survival and security needs of all its members.

In addition to the impact of the formal organization's culture on the development of personality, the employees' membership and acceptance into work groups wields an influence upon the underlying value system of the social organization and the personal objectives and goals of the work group members. The development and growth of personality in this environment reflects commitment to reference groups located either within the formal organization and its managerial hierarchy or within the informal organization of the work group members and the leadership and power positions which characterize that association.

Evidence suggests that through a self-selection process the personnel of the organization will, over a period of time, match the prevailing formal and informal leadership climate. The social culture will exhibit features which are congruent with the personalities of organizational leaders and their definition of its course and direction. As we have already noted, the personalities of the managers of the formal organization reflect leadership styles and managerial philosophies based upon their personal backgrounds and experience.

In today's changing world we frequently find the organization preferring a democratic style of leadership with a managerial philosophy of decentralization and delegation of authority gradually replacing an autocratic style of leadership with a managerial philosophy of centralization and emphasis on centralized authority and responsibility. We can assume, though a change in an individual's personality is slow and gradual, that given a sufficient exposure to a particular type of organizational and leadership climate, his personality will eventually internalize the prevailing values of the culture of the organization and that he will become an integrated part of the mass of employees and managers in the organization. This transformation is also reflected in concerns for the detrimental effects of hierarchical bureaucratic organization on men's creative abilities and their individuality. The demands of conformity, which are designed to assure predictable performance toward the organization's objectives and goals, may lead to the development of organization man or upward mobile man, a person absorbed by the organizational society and deprived of his personal identity.

THE IMPORTANCE OF BUSINESS CULTURE

It is important to recognize that in Western industrialized society a man's most important status position and role relate to his work and his occupation. His occupational position and role establish his niche and enable him to claim a recognized place in society. The occupational position of a man, in fact, determines most of the other positions and roles which may be open to him. Personality in our culture is heavily weighted with an internalization of behavior approved by the business culture. Therefore, a man's organizational environment and the personality of his boss are significant forces in determining the dimensions of a man's personality. Occupational identification grows with the length of his service in the organization in support of its objectives and goals. Likewise, the characteristics of the business culture as defined by the relationship between the manager and the managed are ultimately reflected in the society as a whole and thus become a matter of great importance to all members of the society.

SUMMARY

So far we have discussed personality formation as it relates to the imperatives of culture-status-role influences and to the process of internalizing or learning the values of society. This way of looking at the determinants of human behavior emphasizes visible inputs to the "black box" of personality (X factors in Fig. 1) which are then transformed through unseen, internal processes and lead to visible reactions, responses, or outputs (Z factors in Fig. 1). Behavior, according to this way of thinking is best understood from the point of view of an objective observer who derives cause and effect relationships from an analysis of situational events and observed responses. We turn now to exploring a subjective view of personality formation.

CHAPTER FIVE

THE PILOT CONCEPT OF PERSONALITY

"If we are to study and understand man, we need a human model."

ROLLO MAY

Looking at personality development as a process of acculturation and social-ization suggest to us a robot concept of man. Society provides cultural stimuli (S) which evoke certain responses (R) from its subjects. The growing child (or the learning adult) discovers that if he is caught doing something wrong, he will experience painful consequences. His subsequent behavior changes in order to avoid pain; if the change ends his distress, he accepts it and incorporates it into his behavioral repertoire. On the other hand, when the learner finds that certain ways of acting and even thinking bring him reward from his tutors, he repeats these responses whenever they seem to him to be socially appropriate. The sum of all experience creates habitual patterns and qualities of behavior which give each individual an identity as a person, i.e., a "personality." Accord-ing to this way of looking at human development, the ultimate causes and, there-fore, control of human conduct reside outside the human organism.

Some writers argue that all theorizing and hypothesizing about the human personality should be in terms of relationships between directly observable and, therefore, external variables. They argue that only in this way can the behavioral sciences advance beyond philosophy and become a science. Such inputs and out-puts are tangible and visible phenomena which can be observed, counted, clas-sified, and formed into hypotheses for experimentation, measurement, and interpretation. Human behavior could thus become predictable and, therefore, controllable. Hypothethical constructs, that is, abstractions of mental processes which include nonobservable elements, would not be included in these investigations because their existence and their operation could only be inferred. They are "unscientific." Science can deal, it is asserted, only with data which are public. Subjective processes, or consciousness in the mind of a human being, can be understood only in terms of its inputs and outputs, e.g., words or actions. What he may *feel* about what he does is irrelevant.

This emphasis on the objectively observable inputs and outputs of the human mind helps us to establish important uniformities in man's nature, but this approach is less valuable when it comes to accounting for that which is *unique* in man. We need to move with care from the general to the particular in human relations. Knowing something about people "in general," even though it is based in science, may even impair our understanding of individuals, as Carl Jung and others have pointed out. This is a form of stereotyping which is no less dangerous than "knowing" that all Scotsmen are stingy or that intelligence varies with the color of a person's skin.

We must, therefore, venture beyond the limits of objectivism and scientific method in our search for useable conceptual models which will help us to understand and explain the Y factors in the "black box" of human personality. We caution the reader that in this attempt we enter an area of speculation, joining those of the therapeutic schools who have struggled to understand man in the interests of healing his psychic wounds. Members of these schools argue that concentrating solely on observable aspects of behavior is not enough. Their work with disturbed individuals has shed light on the fact that psychological changes do occur under certain conditions. They focus attention on the importance of the inner workings of a person's mind in the ultimate definition of personality.

It would now be useful to recall our earlier chapters on the nature of man. When we begin to make assumptions or inferences about the workings of the human mind, we are forced to make some basic assumptions about human nature itself. It will be recalled that we discussed the polar assumptions of good and evil and pointed out how taking one assumption or the other affects our concepts of motivation and social control. If we think of personality development as a robot process, we are not concerned with this question because whatever man is and becomes is a product of his physical and social environment. But if we concede that man has the power of choice, we must try to understand what basis he has for piloting his course.

THE FREUDIAN MODEL

One of the first and certainly one of the most important attempts to construct a dynamic model of the human mind was by Sigmund Freud. Although he has been called an "objectivist" because of his biological-historical orientation, we believe that he must be placed with those who emphasize a subjective view of personality. Freud spent his life trying to understand and explain what goes on inside the "black box" of the human mind. The record of his ideas and thought forms the foundation for much of modern psychiatry and psychotherapy, although the neo-Freudians, as discussed earlier, differ with him on significant details. His concepts of a fixed and universal human nature energized by a few, basic drives have objectivistic overtones. However, we believe that his model of the structure and functioning of personality, his "mythology" of the human mind, is important to an understanding of subjectivistic theories, and we therefore introduce them into our discussion at this time.

Freud believed that human behavior can be understood only in relation to the ideas, decisions, and unconscious motives located in the mind and that they ultimately derive their energy from internal, biological drives. The Freudian personality structure consists of three major parts or subsystems, the *id*, the *ego*, and the *superego*. When these systems are functioning in harmonious relationships, the individual is mentally healthy. When they are at odds, there are symptoms of maladjustments in behavior involving other people and things. Freud believed that these maladjustments were caused by some combination of the individual's earlier history, his constitutional endowment, and his present environment. He concluded that overcoming pyschological problems required a longitudinal rather than a cross-sectional approach—an exploration by the psychoanalyst and his client of the history, internal workings, and relationships of the parts of the client's personality. Thus, the clinical practice of psycho-analysis as an approach to repairing a malfunctioning personality developed.

The line between those who are mentally ill and those whose behavior lies in the "normal range" is very hard to define. There are obvious cases of mental illness in which the symptoms are so severe that it is impossible for the individual to carry on useful human relationships. On the other hand, all human personality systems exhibit some behavior inadequacies which may be diagnosed and to some extent, at least, corrected. These personality defects may contribute to inter-personal difficulties arising from inaccurate assumptions about human nature, less effective communication with other people, a poor understanding of how to cope with interpersonal conflict, and a lack in self-awareness and sensitivity toward others. Normalcy in personality is a matter of the degree to which an individual understands and accepts himself, and is in control of himself.

An extensive discussion of Freud's ideas will not be undertaken here. How-ever, because of their relationship to later discussions of the concept of self, a brief and selective description will be outlined at this point. Since we believe it is easier to understand the ego when the other parts of Freud's model of personal-ity have been described, the id and the superego will be discussed first. By the concept of *id*, Freud referred to a bundle of instincts which he subsumed under two broad classifications, the life instincts (sex drives and other needs whose satis-faction relates to man's survival) and the death instincts (manifested in self-destructive, aggressive tendencies which usually turn against others when they encounter the urge to survive). These instincts form the source of internal ten-sions which are constantly striving to achieve release and therefore relief. The id, according to Freud, operates in accordance with the "pleasure principle," that is, it seeks to substitute the more immediate pleasure of release from the tensions of unrequited desires, without regard to the consequences. The *superego* is the expression and the guardian of the individual's moral and ethical systems. It is a manifestation of the individual's early identification with parental morality, punishing him for moral trangressions (conscience) and, at times, causing him to value virtue more than truth or reality (ego-ideal).

For our purposes the *ego* in Freudian theory is perhaps the most important subsystem to explore. This subsystem of personality has been described by Freud as the seat of the personality's executive function. In its initial phases, the ego's development precedes that of the superego. The new-born child, driven by the seething mass of raw, instinctual power in the id, soon discovers that he must find ways of reconciling his urges with the world of men. The ego system evolves in response to this need. Its activity and its decision-making processes, instead of being governed by the "pleasure principle" as is the id, are ruled by what Freud described as the "reality principle." Pleasure and need satisfactions are seen as more certain when reality is taken into account and the actual conditions under which satisfaction can be achieved in the real world are discovered. In this process a great many substitutions and compromises are made and may become the source of conflict in the personality. It is in these transactions which occur between the ego and reality (mainly in the area of interpersonal relations in the individual's experience) that the operational qualities of the personality develop. The growing and developing person experiences his parents and other authority figures and is compelled to cope with such important human needs and emotions as love, affection, esteem, security, power and authority relationships, and others. In this process learnings take place which are incorporated into the person's ego and superego and constitute his characteristic ways of responding to the complex forces and counterforces which arise between his id and the interpersonal world.

As the ego develops in response to the often conflicting demands of the id, and the demands of society reflected in the superego, only a part of ego enters the individual's awareness—that part of it which is in use or which intrudes itself into consciousness at the moment. Another part of the ego is in a preconscious condition; that is, it lies outside awareness as a sort of dormant inventory of ways of thinking, memories, and ideas, but it may be evoked upon demand. Still another part of the ego subsystem lies outside awareness in a more or less inaccessible state which Freud labeled the *unconscious*.

The concept of unconscious motivation has many meanings among psychologists. People respond to different stimuli in different ways. They may act through ignorance or through a more or less conscious and rational process of selective attention. They may decide that certain sources of stimuli are irrelevant to their behavior. They may act automatically in response to the memory of past associations. For example, a person may be only dimly aware of his reasons for deciding to restrict output along with his work group rather than to maximize his output as a matter of personal gain and self-interest. Or a manager might be upset when his opposition to the right of his employees to strike is attributed to his belief in the doctrine of "economic man" rather than to his sense of fairness over wage demands. Another part of the unconscious contains the traces of experiences which occurred at the beginnings of infancy at a time when the ability to symbolize had not been learned. These experiences still affect the personality in various ways, but they can never be called into awareness because they are pre-verbal—the individual has no memory of them.

The unconscious in Freudian theory, however, does not seem to mean any of these things. To Freud, the unconscious was a reservoir of experiences, a reservoir created by defensive acts of choice on the part of the ego. He called this exercise of choice, *repression*. Experiences which are painful and in some way seem to threaten the *ego structure*—that is, attack the effective identification and accommodation systems, the unified, organized responses, which have been worked out by the ego with the real world in response to the id's demands and the superego's controls—are excluded from consciousness. These experiences or urges may originate in the ego, in the id, or in the superego. The decision to banish them to the unconscious regions of the mind is made by the ego as one way of dealing with the feelings of fear or anxiety which accompany them. Though banished from view, they continue to exist in the personality, where they may remain dormant or find expression in another form through other mechanisms of defense.

Children are more vulnerable to the repressive process than adults simply because they lack the experience to cope with perceived threats to the ego structure. When we are young our ego defenses are much more essential to our development than they are as we grow older. So also is affection and support, especially by those nearest to us. In some young people the very nature of their experiences during growth and development results in malfunctioning ego and superego systems and a consequent imbalance in the checking versus the urging forces with which they must cope. Many people thus carry into adulthood a great many repressed fears and anxieties and, without help, never find out that these may be unnecessary and in fact, crippling to their interpersonal effectiveness.

Repressed experiences may be recalled to consciousness or awareness when the individual discovers that the threats which precipitated them no longer exist. If the individual can in some way be brought to re-examine his repressed experiences at a time and under circumstances in which their threatening aspects are reduced or eliminated, he may voluntarily turn the light of consciousness on them and find that he is able to overcome his former anxieties. This phenomenon formed the basis for Freud's theories of behavioral change through psychoanalysis. Self-analysis may help to bring this result about, as discussed by Karen Horney and others, but generally there must be a series of interventions by an outside change agent, a psychotherapist or a person enacting a similar role. In the stabilized personality, the urging and checking forces—that is, the id, on the one hand, and the ego and superego on the other—are in balance. As we shall see, however, many adults are "over-defensed," i.e., their ratio of conscious to unconscious is small relative to what it should be.

INSIDE LOOKING OUT

With this brief outline of Freud's model of human personality as a point of departure, let us look into some more recent ideas concerning the nature of man. The continuing dissatisfaction with an explanation of personality as a mere reflection of societal and cultural influences has led to other significant commentaries on man's personality in our time and a renewed interest in the subjective dimensions of man's inner self, under the assumption of free will rather than determininism.

A number of writers have raised the question of whether the impact of our industrialized and urbanized society is not affecting personality in adverse ways by stressing the superficial needs of conforming to the demands of the organizational society. Such writers believe that objectivistic theories of personality and individual growth place the emphasis on a person's past. However, they assert, this does not provide an adequate explanation. They believe that behavior must also be considered, indeed, cannot be understood at all, except as it is analyzed from the frame of reference of the individual himself. In this view, cause and effect in observed behavior are expressions of the individual's *perceptions* of situational events. This is a pilot view—man's behavior and development are in *process* and are always directed toward self-consistency and self-actualization. Man is *being* and *becoming*, moving constantly ahead, and cannot be wholly understood on the basis of where he has been.

ISOLATION OF THE INDIVIDUAL

Man used to live in what might be characterized as a more natural social environment, in small communities where he earned a livelihood from simple pursuits such as hunting and tilling the soil. The little community or folk society represented stability and security in man's life. Where he was born he knew he would die. His status was established by tradition or represented an emergent occupational role where his specialized talents naturally became available to benefit the whole community. Intimate face-to-face familiarity with all those around him assured each member of the community ease of interaction in a spirit of cooperation, mutual trust, and confidence. Man had little to fear in such an established society, and he could more easily be himself in his daily pursuits and social interactions.

In contrast we live today in an adaptive, mass society. But adaptation is to the coefficient of production and not to the human community. Man is reduced to a cog in the production machinery. He finds himself in his occupational life responsible only for a partial task, and identification with his personal contribution is lost in the final product. Under these circumstances, man becomes estranged and alienated from the technological environment and urban society. There is little possibility for the ordinary person to find himself in his work environment. Nor does urban society provide social support or status definition. Competitive values tend to reduce each person to an isolated individual and throw him on his own resources in establishing relationships for survival.

THE RISE OF ORGANIZATION MAN

As the technological production-oriented society developed, mass production provided the norms and the conditions for the emergence of mass society. Individual creativity no longer had a natural play in an environment governed by standardized job descriptions requiring conforming work performance. The rise of increasingly complex bureaucratic organizations further reduced the human element to an object in a machine-like environment where the focus was on instrumental and utilitarian behavior. Man himself became another man's instrument, and was used to reach the objectives and goals of an organizational collectivity.

Against this background, the rise of the organization man becomes inevitable. The Protestant Ethic, emphasizing individual commitment to work and the assigning of spiritual significance to the battle for survival, has been replaced by a social ethic. The *organization* produces and the *organization* provides security for those who fit into its mold. Swimming with the stream becomes the preferred way of life and work. Conforming and agreeing make the wish to belong come true for faithful members of the group. Progress is at the level of the lowest common denominator among the membership—mediocrity becomes the way of meritocracy. The former inner-directed man working out his own destiny, confident in his personal wisdom, is replaced by the other-directed man whose radar screen returns to him continuous feedback from the work environment as to his group fit. Thus, today's organization man is prone to judge himself according to the value the market places on what he has to offer, the bundle of goods he represents. In turn, he is prone to value others in accordance with the price they might fetch in the marketplace. He will choose to associate with those who go for the highest price. Instead of viewing man as an end he sees man as a means with the conditions of the marketplace governing his social choices.

Accordingly, the question can properly be raised as to whether or not the urban, industrialized mass society has annihilated natural man. The inner self, the personal "I," is evident only to the extent that introspection and self-analysis brings it forth. But the veneer of industrial civilization has almost completely hidden it from view. It is this hidden and latent "I," this "I" which in final analysis *is* personality in its innermost dimension, that has become the object of intense interest among those who would formulate a theory of personality more applicable to the man of today.

THE ROGERIAN VIEW

An example of a subjectivistic theory of personality is found in the writings of Carl Rogers. In Rogers' view, the individual is the center of experience, some of which he is aware of and some of which he finds too painful to admit to awareness. His primary objective is to actualize and maintain himself, that is, to move toward the fullest expression of his potentialities for maturity and to defend himself against physical and psychological threats. All man's behavior is, therefore, goal-directed by means which he, himself, defines. Hence, in Rogers' view, an individual's behavior is best understood from that individual's frame of reference and must include an understanding of his goals.

The self, according to Rogers, is expressed by the consistent pattern of values and relationships with others which emerges in awareness as the individual moves from one experience to another. As experiences occur they are (1) incorporated into the self-structure if they seem to be consistent with the self-concept, (2) "ignored" if they seem unrelated to the self, or (3) "denied" to awareness or admitted only in "distorted" form if they seem inconsistent with the self-structure. Psychological tensions occur in the personality whenever experiences are denied to awareness. But psychological adjustment takes place when the self is open to experience, that is, has greater tolerance for experience. The more that experience is denied to awareness, the more rigid the self-structure becomes and the less understanding and acceptant of others the individual becomes. The kinship is clear between these ideas and Freud's concepts of the ego structure, the conscious and unconscious minds, and the mechanisms of defense.

Thus, Rogers emphasizes the unity of the individual, and views optimistically the individual's capacity for making "good" choices. In these views, of course, he joins A. H. Maslow and the several neo-Freudians we discussed in an earlier chapter. The central themes that seem to characterize these theories, which seek a new concept of man, are holistic and phenomenological in that they emphasize introspection and see man and environment as one; they reflect an existential philosophy of man.

THE EXISTENTIAL QUESTION

The traditional view of the world and of objects in it has tended to follow early Greek thought that essence precedes existence. In other words, prefabrications exist in the form of ideas which represent the true nature of all phenomena, including the true nature of man. All one needs to do to measure the nature of anything is to match it with its preconception. This theory has resulted in an emphasis on rationalism and a belief that the functioning of the world can be logically explained. The *idea* is given precedence over the *object* it represents. To the extent that the object conforms to the idea of the object, to that extent it is more nearly perfect. In religious life, for example, God has represented man's essence, and man approaches perfection the more he approaches the idea of God in action and deed.

In contrast to this philosophy, the existentialists believe that the viewpoint of rationalism with its emphasis on the philosophical idea is useless. It does not serve even as a palliative to modern man who is progressively being crushed under the weight of a production- and power-oriented society. The requirements of the production process reduce industrial man to little more than an impersonality, like a chair or a table or any other inanimate object.

The philosophical background of the phenomenological or subjectivistic view of man is most clearly expressed in modern existentialism. Existentialists believe that existence must come before essence. Man's life tends towards absurdity if it conforms to arbitrary conventions and rules—as if he were to live forever—when in fact his is only a temporary existence and sooner or later he must face death. Man's most precious quality is in *being*. He has the potential to define himself "free," and he should do so. He cannot take recourse in excuses for actions he has taken and later regretted. He is responsible for himself, and whatever he experiences in his existence, his being and becoming. In short, his actions are his existence and thus his person. Only after action has confronted reality does the *idea* in the Greek sense exist and assume a meaningful definition.

Hence, the existentialist view is that man is responsible for what he is and becomes. It looks at the totality of man and environment and considers what the individual can do to bring meaning into his life, what the conditions of existence really are, and what man can do, in his own terms, to make life a more significant and rewarding experience. To this seeking for a meaning, at least in the positive view, what exists is not judged by prior standards but by whatever is needed to *be* and to *become* in a responsible and need-satisfying way. Because man is conscious of himself as an integral and specific part of his experience, he is capable of making choices—of defining and selecting courses of action. Environment may limit his choices in the way that the shape of the mountain determines one's path on its slopes, but environment does not define behavior. As a goal-seeking being, man always will make choices which seem to him to actualize or contribute to the development or nurture of his potentialities.

In this view, an individual exists *before* we can determine what he is. He is, therefore, a *product* of his experience. He has no essence—that is quality or character—which antecedes his being and existence. The subjective view of personality, according to existential philosophy, reflects man's interaction with his environment in terms of the "inner man" looking out, developing self and self-awareness—a subject-object rather than an object alone. This embodies "I"—a concept rooted in man's assumed freedom to act. Paraphrasing Descartes, we can say the starting point is "I act, therefore, I am."

The theme of existential philosophy in its more optimistic aspects is interwoven with the Freudian objective of improving man's lot through his personal involvement in the search for understanding and change. In a similar fashion, it complements the subjectivistic theories of Carl Rogers and the neo-Freudians. In the past the Protestant Ethic provided a philosophical underpinning for man's work life; the new generations clearly are drawn to the Existential Ethic.

Before we move ahead, however, we need to make a distinction between the personality as a whole, with which we have been concerned up to this point, and the "self," that part of the mind which rules the individual in interpersonal relations. Personality represents the totality of a person's characteristics—his attitudes, needs, traits, abilities, feelings, and other mental processes. The concept of personality includes both the idea of man as a robot, i.e., one who is molded in the course of interacting with others, and man as a pilot, i.e., a self-conscious being with goals, values, and the pre-eminence of will or choice as a factor in his conduct. The concept of self is derived from the fact that man has the capacity to become an object to himself and thus to have attitudes toward himself in relation to others. He has ideas about his personal traits, feelings about various aspects of himself in different situations, and a tendency to act toward himself and toward others in a variety of rational and irrational ways. It is these ideas, feelings, and ways of behaving which constitute his self, his "unique imprint" upon the roles and positions he assumes in society. In the next chapter we will examine this concept in detail.

CHAPTER SIX

THE INTERPERSONAL SELF

"I play according to the rules of the game, to preserve my prestige and feeling of superiority and merit."

H. S. SULLIVAN

In business organizations as well as in other groups we spend a great deal of time speculating about what lies behind another person's mask, what "hidden agenda" is influencing his behavior, and to what extent we really know one another. We are aware that some people seem more distant, more unfathomable than others. We are also aware that we feel freer to open up our own deeper feelings and thoughts to some rather than to others. In our formalistic society the subjective side of human relations and our concept of self tend to be de-emphasized, and yet we know that these aspects of human nature play an important part in human behavior and, therefore, in whatever understanding we may attain of our fellow man.

Some of us, including many (if not most) of those who manage organizations, adopt the view that human motives are inscrutable and that man's behavior can best be studied and controlled in terms of external, i.e., observable incentives and responses. Those who take this point of view tend to play down the role of subjective choices. They study man as an object and seek to discover the forces around him which cause his behavior. Consequently, they emphasize man's general adaptability and pay little attention to individual continuity and consistency in behavior from situation to situation. To them, man is essentially a robot, responding and responsive more or less automatically to the push and pull of events. They think of control of individual and social behavior, therefore, in terms of an individual's reaction to common physiological stimuli or to such impersonal externalities as rules, laws, traditions, authority, and power.

At the opposite extreme are those who argue that man's behavior is determined mainly through the perceptions, interpretations, and motivations located in his mind. Those who emphasize a subjective view believe that the key to understanding how he responds to his environment is to be found within individual man. They tend, therefore, to think of him more as a pilot, steering his own course through life's exigencies. They are concerned with the constancies in an individual's behavior over time and see control of behavior as a function, primarily, of individual choice and an expression of personal values and attitudes.

The truth would seem to lie somewhere between. If we think of man as a robot, we cannot explain his individuality, his uniqueness, his creative contributions to society. If, on the other hand, we think of man as a pilot, we cannot explain his social nature which rests on cooperation with his fellow man under the influence of a common culture. In order to make sense of human nature we need to think of man as a product of both his environment, i.e., the culturally defined roles he plays, and something else, some internal structure, some intervening control, which we cannot see. This "something else" is hypothesized by us to be the individual's concept of himself, what he knows about himself, what sort of person he thinks he is, and what kind of person he thinks he ought to be. In order to analyze behavior, therefore, we must consider not only the environment in which the actor acts but also the subjective processes which occur in his mind and, especially, the interpersonal relationships which he experiences. By focusing on a product of these relationships, the interpersonal self, it is possible to develop a conceptual scheme for understanding the behavior of man.

THE EMERGENCE OF SELF

The self-concept, the "something" beneath our skin which affects our behavior, is an organization of ideas about ourselves which we derive from our experience with others. Throughout our lives we are concerned with being approved by others.

From earliest childhood we reach out for the affection of people who are important to us. In this process, we build a concept in our minds of behavior which seems to lead to acceptance and love. This emerging pattern gradually becomes a conscious synthesis or mental image of what we are and what we think we are to other people. The process begins as we start to differentiate ourselves from the environment. It can be traced to the initial emergence of personal boundaries which appear as we experience objects that we conclude are not part of us. As these experiences continue, we acquire a sense of being something apart from the environment, of being a separate object, with dimensions, movement, bodily characteristics, sounds—a "thing" having particularity and essence. At the same time, we discover a private world of the mind which becomes identified as the home of our feelings, sensations, thoughts, choices, and decisions.

Thus, in our discovery of the environment and in our realization that other people exist and have attitudes which affect us, we begin to become persons. We learn the meaning of physical and mental pain and anguish, and the power of reward and punishment. We discover ways of behaving which bring us pleasure instead of pain, affection and approval instead of hostility and rejection. We become aware of a private and special identity comprising values, attitudes, and goals, an ideology or frame of reference through which we evaluate not only ourselves but other people.

One of the chief characteristics or qualities of this self structure is the consistency which characterizes it through time. There seems to be at work within each of us a core of organized energy which, from a personal point of view, gives to our behavior a coherent, viable pattern. In brief, we accept ideas and experiences which seem to us to be compatible with our self-concept and reject or in some way reform or alter those which are not.

When we face problems or situations which seem to threaten our growing sense of unity, we experience feelings of uneasiness or anxiety which alert us to the need to defend ourselves. These problems or situations may stem from external sources, that is, we may be menaced by some person or object, or they may arise from internal conflicts. We may, for example, feel apprehensive that some impulse or craving within ourselves will cause us to do something which will bring punishment from others. Or we may experience conflicts with our conscience or moral self which fill us with mental anguish. Consider the following illustration.

I find that there are feelings which I am unable to accept and respond to as I experience them. They make me anxious, and if I cannot cope with them according to their real nature I am on the verge of losing control over myself. Without knowing that I do so, I blame the problem on someone or something else. "I feel that I am to blame," becomes "I feel that he is making me feel guilty"—or I cover my feelings of hatred with exaggerated "love." Thus I offer one kind of behavior for another as a cover-up or I simply refuse to engage myself at all, preferring to avoid my anxiety by slipping off into a dream world of fantasy or returning in thought to some act of my childhood which had brought me comfort in the face of danger.

Thus, while a part of our behavior reflects a realistic knowledge of ourselves, another part consists of hiding behind façades where we neither know ourselves nor do we permit others to know us. This behavior is self-protecting because it enables us to relegate unpleasant experiences to subconscious levels while we are enjoying and projecting relative security at conscious levels. However, while self-protecting behavior helps to make life tolerable and brings a kind of stability to our relationships with others, it may also result in a major orientation toward "one-way" thinking and behaving and give us little understanding or feeling for better alternatives. In other words, the walls we build for protection may also act as barriers to learning, making it impossible to recognize personal shortcomings which need our attention. Out of our subjective world we call forth a variety of images which enable us to vary our behavior as we deal with persons in the different social situations we encounter. We don masks to fit the occasion, projecting social selves we hope other people will see and approve. In this each one of us is both subject and object, both "I" and "Me," and the difficulty is that these two dimensions of ourselves can never be quite the same. Let us consider this concept from a personal viewpoint.

As somebody looks at me, I am reduced to an object in his presence, and, depending on his knowledge of me, this object will take on a certain definition in his mind. But I, in turn, will be quite convinced that on the one hand he has not been able to fathom the whole of me, and on the other hand that, in fact, I do not know all the dimensions of his definition of me. If I discover that he really expects a certain quality in me, or if I believe that in order to satisfy my desire to please him, my "me" must have a certain quality, I may deliberately attempt to add it to my social self, to his concept of me, though I cannot be sure how successfully I have done so.

However, it is clear that I can never be sure that my own concept of what I am, looking at myself objectively, as though from without, matches that of another viewing me. Nor can I be sure that what I, subjectively, believe I am projecting is an accurate image of what others see. I am aware that I can never confidently say that I have a completely exhaustive definition of either of these dimensions of my self. For the feedback I receive from others is imperfect, and the deeply buried traces of my past experiences and the imperatives of my biology seem to pop up at unexpected times and places to influence and distort what I see.

We are, therefore, creatures of many selves, inner and outer, internal and external, each influencing the other in many patterns and ways. Taken together at any moment in time and place, they give us our personal quality and define us as a person. In an effort to improve our understanding of their mutual dependence and variety, let us now consider in some detail the subjective and objective elements of our selves.

THE PERSONAL SELF OR "I"

Our personal self is what we believe we are, and want to be. It contains all our expectations and aspirations, all our dreams, and all our secret wishes. It is the self we know the best but may fear to reveal and expose to attack or alteration. To help us hide parts of this inner self, we set up various kinds of psychological defenses. These sometimes force us into neurotic yearnings for affection, aggressions against our fellows, or lonely isolation. Our dilemma is that, while these excursions help to preserve us from emotional defeat, we can never simultaneously know what or who we are if we are not free to be ourselves and thus to discover ourselves. We are prisoners of our apprehensions and chained in the struggle never to deviate from what is "normal" and "accepted." Consequently we can be accused of finding our comfort and maintaining our equilibrium in conformist submission to rules created by others.

On the other hand, our personal self may assume the role of a protecting force standing between us and the socializing process. Where it is not overwhelmed through identification with others, it is individuality—the expression of the uniqueness of our person as contrasted with the common attitudes and values which we share with others. This is the avaricious and unscrupulous Jacob, who with trickery and deceit, purloined Esau's birthright for a "mess of pottage." Or it is the stormy, defiant Beethoven raging against tradition and protesting the musical values of his time.

Our personal or subjective self is an adapting mechanism like the ego. Freud tied our basic motivational patterns to innate biological urges which are harmonized with the social order through the ego. The personal self or "I," as conceived in this discussion, is the means by which we learn to live cooperatively with others within the culture *while striving to achieve the fullest development of our own personality and capacities.* In our view the difference is important. This concept of the personal self is positive and constructive in its thrust rather than negative and remedial.

Our personal self, then, is the mental reflection of all our past experience. It includes those characteristics and qualities which distinguish us from all other individuals. It includes all that we have learned and accepted as a part of ourself. It also includes all the repressed experiences or unconscious motivations which affect our behavior in ways of which we are unaware. From this internal vantage point we idealize all the various roles we play in life, that is, we assume the characteristics or qualities each one of us would like to think he represents to the world.

THE SOCIAL SELF OR "ME"

The way we appear to others and the way we *think* we appear to others are parts of the phenomenon which constitute the social self or "me." If we are to understand something about our social selves we must somehow step outside our skin and try to see ourselves as the object others see. This, of course, means that we must attempt to assume the points of view of others and try to imagine what they see and how they feel about us. For reasons to be explained, we can never be completely successful in this attempt.

Potentially, each of us produces as many external images as there are others involved. This would create a very complex range of social selves if we did not share a common culture with others and consequently at least some common interpretations of experience. This consensus makes it possible for them and for us to derive a composite impression or synthesis of our "observable self." Clearly, if it were not for this phenomenon of shared perceptions among individuals, communication and understanding would be impossible. In dealing with groups these syntheses are absolutely necessary if man is to achieve social efficiency. In dealing with individuals, however, deviation from the general pattern is equally essential. The hazards as well as the necessities of stereotyping need to be recognized. One of the disadvantages of science is that it generalizes a class or type of phenomena; it does not account for the individual case. This is a major drawback in medicine and psychotherapy where the individual case is the crucial focus of concern. It is likwise a problem in organizations when a particular individual or a particular small group may be the focus of concern.

Our social self also reflects the influence of expectations which others have concerning our behavior, expectations of both a social and a psychological nature. Social expectations involve norms and values to which, for social effectiveness, we must be sensitive and to which our overt behavior must in large measure respond. Psychological expectations are concerned with the whole question of motivation and are closely related to individual needs. Perhaps we can define the social self in the following way.

When I know what other people expect, I can try to integrate myself with the social situation by being a "normal" person in that situation as this is defined by others. This part of me is the part I want to and find myself willing to set forth in my behavior or what, because it is my habitual way, I want to be. The role that I play is therefore a reflection of my inner self as I operationalize it in my actions. It is also a mirror image of what I believe others expect from me and what I believe is essential if I am to avoid rejection or disapproval.

In an organizational context, expectations would include both the meaning which subordinates have assigned to the behavior of their superior and the norms or standards by which his behavior is judged. Only by taking the attitudes of others can the superior see himself as others see him and thus understand the meaning of his actions as they are experienced by others. Only those "others" can interpret his behavior objectively. If what he wishes to convey is not accurately perceived by others, then the meaning he wishes to give to his actions is distorted. Similarly, it is only through an external frame of reference that we can know the attitudes of others and thus become acceptable and effective members of a social group.

Thus, there exist differences in the external modes of the self, and these differences have a significant effect upon our ways of relating to other people. Our own view of how others perceive us and how others actually do perceive us may and, of course, usually does overlap. On occasion, however, these views may be so divergent, so incompatible, as not to coincide at all. The more they overlap the more we find our communications in harmony with those of other people, and the more accurate we can therefore be in our definition of social situations. As self and other perceptions move apart, we become less and less able to define accurately what we and others are doing to each other in our interpersonal encounters. The danger in too much overlap is that we may go so far that we lose our identity and become a social robot; if there is too little overlap, we may find ourselves adrift and out of contact with the world of reality.

We can summarize our discussion of self so far by emphasizing its dual nature. We find that we have some views of our self which, in a sense, are private and personal. Like the secret lives of Walter Mitty in Thurber's novels, these views sometimes have the quality of fantasy; they are what we expect and want to be, what we like to think we are. These views are also very real, in the sense that they affect our behavior and consequently all our relationships with other people. However, we are also aware, some of us more than others, that other people have views of us which differ from our private views, and that our conduct is influenced by their views, as well. The self, then, is composed of these two major parts, the personal and the social, which differ but which are interdependent.

THE RELATIONSHIP OF THE PARTS OF THE SELF

Now let us examine, in schematic form, the various parts of the self system we have been describing, and explore the various ways in which the personal and social modes relate to each other. We can think of the stream of situational events which go to make up our objective experience or "reality" as culture or input, the intervening and unobservable processes of the mind as a construct of our personal self, and the output as our social self or the person others see in us. Thus we have a simple model of the total self system which includes the fundamental premise that man is both a robot, an objective social product, and a pilot, a subjective product of the human will. We need both concepts in synthesis in order to understand the nature of self and the function of self-awareness and self-acceptance in man's interpersonal world.

In Fig. 2 the personal-social self system is shown as consisting of four basic parts: (1) inputs from the culture, e.g., learned behaviors and products of behavior; (2) the personal self; (3) the social self; and (4) an interaction-feedback loop. In the personal-self or "I" component, the area labelled A represents consciousness or awareness. Following our analogy to classical ego psychology, this area includes our personal and private values, thoughts, feelings, ideas, and memories. The area B includes similar mental categories which lie below the level of consciousness, i.e., are unconscious. The dotted lines represent the ego defenses, some of which stand between us and our environment while others form an

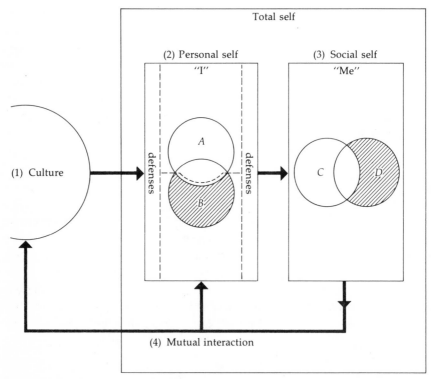

(2) Personal and private values, thoughts,
feelings, ideas, and memories:

A Conscious   *B* Unconscious

(3) Social self as seen by

C Me   *D* Others

Fig. 2.   Diagram of personal-social self system.

internal filter between the conscious and unconscious parts of our personality. The defense mechanisms, themselves being involuntary, are also unconscious. A portion of *A* is preconscious, containing mental data which is recallable on demand. The overlap between *A* and *B* represents the outcome of experiences which have, in effect, pushed back the boundary of the unconscious.

In the social-self component, the area marked *C* represents that part of the image of ourselves, or "me," as we think we appear to others. This mental image is not included with other mental images contained in area *A* because we have here, in effect, stepped outside ourself in an effort to obtain an "objective" view of how we seem to others. It is not, therefore, a wholly private view but rather a "looking-glass" self, a product of our assumption of another's perception of us. However, since we cannot completely escape from ourself, we can never fully know what others see in us. Thus, the shaded area of *D* represents aspects of ourself or "me" which can be seen by others but not by us. Similarly, the overlapping portion of *C* and *D* contains aspects of ourself which overlap, that is, on which we and others agree.

The feedback loop marked "mutual interaction" arises from the premise that the external or social self is both a product of and an influence upon the culture and the personal self, as a component of personality. Our behavior is a response to what we have learned, i.e., what we have received from the culture, our own private and unique organization of experience, and the ways in which we find other people responding to us.

SOME PROPOSITIONS ABOUT THE INTERPERSONAL SELF

On the basis of the schematic representation given in Fig. 2 and our previous discussion, we can now set forth a number of propositions or hypotheses concerning the self system and its effect on interpersonal behavior, that is, on our face-to-face relationships with others.

1. There emerges from our inner experience over time an awareness of self as subject and object.

We acquire an inner core of consistent beliefs and feelings about the kind of person we truly are. "I am tall, strong, and intelligent, but I find that some people bore me and some do not like me." This is a subjective view. We also can imagine how we appear to others and what others think of us, and we have feelings about this objective view which affect our behavior. Furthermore, others see us as an object with certain characteristics, only part of which we can know about from their reactions. Their attitudes also affect our behavior.

2.   *Self-awareness and self-acceptance are the same.*

This proposition relates to the principle of consistency which characterizes the self-concept. Experiences which are self-confirming, i.e., are consistent with the personal symbolic identity we carry in our minds, enter consciousness. Those which do not are excluded or transformed by our defenses. To be aware, therefore, is to accept—since we cannot know or be aware of aspects of ourselves unless we want to know them. This does not mean, of course, that we cannot tolerate negative or unpleasant personal experiences. We can, as long as they are consistent with our self as perceived, i.e., we can take the "bad-me" and the "good-me," but we cannot tolerate "not-me."

3.   *Self-awareness in its subjective or personal mode is a function of the ratio between the conscious and unconscious parts of the self.*

The more of our experience we include in our conscious world, the more of ourselves we have learned to recognize and accept, and the lower is our need for self-defense against experience. Referring to Fig. 2, we can express this relationship as $SA_s = A/B$, where SA_s is the subjective dimension of self-awareness, A is the conscious, and B the unconscious part of the self-structure. All our evasive predispositions or defensive behaviors taken together determine the extent to which our personal self is "open"—i.e., receptive to experience. Openness of personal self is characterized by a relationship of trust and confidence between the individual and his social environment. Such an individual is able to receive a large flow of information and communication from others. In contrast, a "closed" personal self mistrusts and is suspicious of the environment. For this individual the flow of information is restricted and flexibility of action is difficult.

4.   *Self-awareness in its objective or social mode is a function of the congruence which exists between our definition of the image we project and our projected image as it is defined by others.*

To the extent that we are independent of the need to protect ourselves, to that extent we can remove our masks and open ourselves to others. This relationship, with reference to Fig. 2, could be expressed as $SA_o = C/D$, where SA_o is the objective dimension of our awareness of our social self, C is the self we think others see, and D is the self others actually see in us.

5.   *The personal and social modes of self-awareness are interdependent.*

The better we know "I," the better we can know "Me." This follows from Proposition 3. The more we know and accept of our inner selves, the less we need to cover up, the less deluded we are about the image we project to others, and the less our unconscious influences the image others see. On the other hand, to know ourselves requires that we reveal ourselves to others in order that they may reflect back what we ourselves cannot see. This follows from Proposition 4. This relationship could be expressed as $SA_s \leftrightarrow SA_o$, where SA_s is the subjective and SA_o is the objective dimension of self-awareness. Referring back to Propositions 3 and 4, we can see that as A, the conscious part of the self, increases relative to B, the unconscious, we become more open to ourselves. As this occurs, C, the social self we perceive, increases relative to D, the social self others perceive, and we become more open to others. The keys to these congruences are *self-disclosure* and *self-acceptance*, and each supports the other. If we are able to open ourselves, that is, reveal inner thoughts and feelings to others, we can gain perspectives about ourselves which would not otherwise be available to us. We can, for example, (1) reveal needs which have been suppressed, (2) open for examination distortions of past experiences which affect our current behavior, (3) discover ways in which we are alike and ways in which we differ from others (finding that others share some feelings with us is a way of relieving anxiety and "shutting off" defenses), (4) develop new interpretations of experience, and (5) *be* ourselves by behaving more nearly in accordance with our potentials.

Self-disclosure and self-acceptance, however, are by no means easy. Both involve uncomfortable forms of self-disparagement. Humility is an uneasy virtue in the western world. In order to disclose our private thoughts and feelings to others, we may have to reveal that we have sometimes deceived others for the sake of expediency. And in order to accept what may be revealed and reflected by others about ourselves may require that we alter a self-concept which has seemed to us to be a comfortable, coherent, and unified link to the world of reality. This leads to a sixth proposition:

6. *The maintenance of self-consistency is a basic motivating force.*

There is in each of us a purposive striving to maintain the consistency or our self-concept. Our interpersonal behavior is governed by a need to preserve the mental image we have of the kind of person we are and the kind of person we are trying to be. From the time when we were children we have learned to practice duplicity by projecting an image to others which *we think those others want us to have.* Maintaining the coherence of this image becomes a way of life—a way of adjusting to the demands of society. This is a primary motive in our behavior and is, therefore, like other motives, an explanation of behavior. It implies that the self is an organized, dynamic system composed of parts related to one another— abilities, needs, drives, instincts, values, interests, traits, social attitudes, pathological trends, and others—and like all systems, it strives to maintain equilibrium in its environment. In short, it persists and is difficult to change.

Let us put this another way. Two or more things which occur together but do not seem to belong together or fit together are experienced as incongruent. If a person knows something about himself and something about his environment which do not seem to him to be compatible, he feels anxiety and becomes aware of a discordant note in his experiencing. An individual may see himself as competent yet suffer repeated failures in his area of supposed competency. Knowledge of such contradictions is disturbing; the self-image and the reality are neither congruent nor harmonious.

When we encounter such feelings of inconsistency in our ideas or motives or experiences, we behave in ways, often unconsciously, which we believe will reduce or eliminate them. If the house we wish to purchase is too costly, we look for a cheaper one, or we buy it and tighten our belts, or we ask the boss for a raise. Or if we think of ourselves as honest, but we are caught stealing cookies, we either (1) revise our view of ourself (a difficult thing to do), (2) refuse to admit that taking a cookie is "stealing," or (3) blame our behavior on something or someone else—"Frankie said it was OK," "Mother only gave me one cookie for supper and Frankie two." In each case, the motivating force is derived from our sense of the fitness of things in relation to our concept of self.

There is always the danger, however, that we will carry the maintenace of self-consistency too far. The expurgated self we present to others may be so at variance with our inner self, or "I", that we lose our individuality and become robot-like, conforming to the wishes and demands of others. This leads to another proposition:

7.   *Where our social self is our prime concern and where our personal self understands and accepts only another's social self, the result is conformity.*

This proposition suggests that we may at times neglect to look beyond the surface of the other's social self. In the process we may suppress our own personal self in preference for conformity with the other's social self, as we experience it. Note that this also follows from Proposition 5, which indicates that self-acceptance and its implications are prerequisites to any understanding of another's personal self. We may conclude that the "organization man" is an easier and safer role for us to assume. We consider ourselves an object, a sort of puppet attached to strings which, as we dance to the puppeteer's commands, brings us popularity, vocational success, prestige, and the attainment of similar goals. When we treat ourselves as objects, we treat others in the same way and, as this proposition indicates, "I" becomes subordinate to "Me". The result is that we abandon personal identity, become desensitized to experience, and subconsciously view ourselves and others as subhuman automatons.

OPENNESS TO EXPERIENCE AS A KEY TO INTERPERSONAL EFFECTIVENESS

The several propositions outlined in this chapter suggest that self-awareness, like the self, is a product of interpersonal relationships. The self emerges over time as we interact with the people who are important to us. Since the way is not always smooth, we fashion a self-structure which seems to us to suit the quality of our human experience. At times, and for some more often than for others, the need to avoid unhappy relationships and the need to live up to our own developing standards evokes a system of unconscious protective behavior which helps us to preserve our emerging self-concept. Where the need for such behavior is great, our awareness of self is reduced and our interpersonal difficulties increase. In addition, we become more closed off from others as the barriers and escapes are built. We are, therefore, increasingly unable to reveal ourselves, and we are cut off from knowledge of ourselves through the corresponding lack of feedback from others. All too often, in order to solve our dilemma, we either abandon our individuality or take refuge in flight from meaningful human relationships. We may become an overbearing lion, superior but lonely, or an obsequious mouse whose frail squeaks cannot be heard above the roar of the crowd.

CHAPTER SEVEN

LEADERSHIP, COOPERATION, AND COMMUNICATION

"Speech which goes from one to another between two natures, and, what is worse, between two experiences, is doubly relative."

ROBERT LOUIS STEVENSON

Leadership involves gaining another's cooperation through the communication process. At an earlier point in our discussion, we suggested that essentially cooperation is inseparable from the quality of the interpersonal relationships which exist between individuals. *Cooperation, communication*, and the *process of change* must be regarded as inextricably bound to one another and to the practice of leadership in modern society. In this and the following chapter we will explore these ideas further, distinguishing between cooperation which is coerced and cooperation which is volunteered, and describing in some detail the communication process and how it affects relationships which concern cooperation and behavioral change.

Let us consider for a moment the following situation:

Carrying the rough sketches of a complicated wing device he had just received from an engineering group, a draftsman working the night shift in a large aircraft plant approached his supervisor.
"What's going on here, Frank? This is the third batch of sketches we've received tonight from B section! They're asking for finished drawings by Thursday! We can't take on this extra work! What do they think we are, anyway?"

This incident illustrates all the elements we mentioned above related to change.

First, there is an appeal for help in solving what appears to be a vexing problem. Second, there is an attitude expressed by the draftsman which, in the response which follows, must either be ignored or changed if cooperation, whether compelled or volunteered, is to be achieved. Finally, the achievement of cooperation will be an outcome of the communication which takes place between the supervisor, representing leadership and authority, and the draftsman as a subordinate. Let us examine some of the broader elements of the situation.

COORDINATION AND COOPERATION

We noted earlier Adam Smith's historic analysis of the competitive instincts in human nature. As we suggested, a closer reading of Smith shows he recognized that self-interest and the good of society are inseparable. Smith assumed that man's self-interest would be governed by moral principles. Every man is motivated by self-interest, but as he promotes his own interests he depends upon the assistance of others. We can see this clearly if we consider the great underlying principle of industrialization, the specialization of labor or division of work. When each man produces only a part of the whole, then each must cooperate with others in order that the whole may be fitted together from individual or group contributions. If one man makes the rim, another the hub, and a third the spokes, then the number and fit of each part, their transfer from one station to another in the assembly phases, and the responsibility for the finished wheel must be coordinated and shared by all the specialists involved.

The idea of specialization of labor has traditionally been related to the production function—the production of a particular good or service. Specialization of labor underlies the traditional ordering of positions through the horizontal division of work and the vertical layering of authority and accountability. Managers and the managed are bound together by the division of work and an imperative of cooperation.

Chester Barnard argued that management's concern must focus on coordination if the organization's objectives and goals are to be realized. Coordination can be achieved only if managers are successful in gaining cooperation from the social organization. Ideally, the sentiments and the behavior of the social organization complement the coordination which was structurally designed into the organization by management. Cooperation reflects acceptance by the employees of the organization's objectives and goals and implies an accommodation by management to at least some important employee goals. However, cooperation is not always complementary to these purposes. It may and often does, in fact, hinder or even nullify the coordination of activities by the organization. For example, it may meet the social needs of a dissident group, but be antithetical to the organization's mission.

We must emphasize that it is not necessarily the mutual interests of the manager and the managed which elicit cooperative behavior. It is their individual and separable interests. Cooperation at the interpersonal level always involves individual differences. The values of the manager will differ from those of the managed and thus their goals will differ. There seems to be little possibility that they will merge or become wholly fused. They need only be compatible with the organization's goals. Since the manager establishes the goals of the organization, he has a proprietary interest in their achievement. This achievement, in fact, is closely associated with his own satisfactions. Most of those who execute the manager's design have no such direct interest in organizational goals. They are more concerned with personal or group goals and satisfactions. They may, in fact, be only vaguely aware of the nature of the organization's goals. Consequently, there may be competition between the interests of managers and managed. Thus managers need special skills to achieve the coordination of task and the cooperation of individuals which will result in effective unity of effort.

Unfortunately, cooperation is not always fully achieved even by those who are aware of its instrumental value in organizational relationships. Cooperation is based upon mutual feelings of trust, friendship, attachment, and interest between individuals. For both parties, these feelings are a result of and are augmented by self-awareness and sensitivity to each other and to the situation requiring cooperation. Cooperation requires, in addition, knowledge of the processes of communication and of personal change through re-learning or re-education. Except in balanced transactions between individuals, involving an exchange of equivalent values, the use of power in personal relationships is not a satisfactory source of cooperation. If the individual who is subject to another's power gains less from the transaction than the wielder of power—that is, if a person is forced to do something where he believes his personal return in the form of some value is less than he perceives as fair and equitable—a deficit is created which affects adversely his willingness to contribute to the common purpose.

Authority adheres to the positions resulting from the horizontal and vertical division of work in the organization, but power is a distinctly personal phenomenon. Specialization creates a power differential among individuals because each specialist achieves superiority within his field of operation through practice and experience. The exercise of functional power or leadership is, therefore, a reciprocal process. It is based upon the conscience of the leader who has at his disposal not only the possibility of rewarding faithful performance but also of punishing those guilty of disobedience. "The strongest," said Rousseau, "is never strong enough to be always master, unless he transforms his strength into right, and obedience into duty." The holder of power attempts to legitimize it by reaching for a position of authority commensurate with the position of power his personal abilities have created. Where the coercive aspect of power becomes predominant in the pursuit of the objectives and goals of the powerful, and fear is the order of the day, then power is naked force and is based upon hate rather than love. This is true whether power resides in the manager, or, as illustrated in the case of some union power, in the managed.

Constructive relationships that exist between members of an organization or with others outside may involve competition. Fair competition is regarded in our society as a social value because it has emerged as an important means by which society makes allocation of scarce resources among competing needs. Thus, competition between individuals and groups within the organization may be healthy if it results in a contribution to efficient performance both by the individual members of the organization and by the organization as a whole.

Such competition can enhance the achievements of the organization and provide for the continued growth and development of its members. However, unfettered competition is not always desirable because it does not guarantee equitable discrimination among competitors, nor the just allocation of resources. In fact, it may slow down the entire enterprise. But it may be the best alternative available short of regimented authority and control. The value of competition may also be seriously questioned if it is superceded in our society by considerations of just distribution of output where conditions of affluence and human and environmental balance outweigh growth on society's value scale.

Intra-organizational competition becomes destructive when it involves relationships between individuals and groups at the interfaces of complementary tasks. Competition and conflict then are clearly out of place because mutual assistance between members or an integration of their knowledge and skills is essential to offset the results of specialization. In such instances cooperation transcends and excludes competition. Nevertheless, managers often set the stage for intergroup conflict by using systems of measurement and reward which emphasize group boundaries rather than the flow of cooperative effort across such boundaries.

Cooperation may be achieved in a variety of ways. As we noted, coercive power is one means. This policy, however, may elicit reactive rather than active responses, little or no self-identification or investment in the object of cooperation, and therefore something less than satisfactory performance. Another way of achieving a cooperative relationship is through an appeal to loyalty. Loyalty is a value in our culture and since it involves the social incentive to conform, it provides a wider base for positive activity and a more personal relationship between one member of an organization and another than does a relationship based on power differences. Still another way to achieve cooperation is through an appeal to conscience. Since conscience is an element of the superego system and has the power to punish (like the parents from whom it came), it can bring to bear strong internalized controls. An appeal may also be made to pride; i.e., to the individual's ego ideal or idealized image. This is a more powerful appeal than the appeal to conscience because it brings an increase in self-esteem as a reward for success rather than simple avoidance of punishment in case of failure, and therefore has positive rather than negative implications. The phenomenal success of industrialization in Japan and competitive performance in the world markets after World War II have been related to the presence of a combination of loyalty, appeal to conscience, and pride.

COMMUNICATION AND COOPERATION

A more powerful form of cooperation is one that is based on a mutually supportive relationship in which each person recognizes that the other has legitimate needs he can satisfy and, in turn, perceives the other as a means of satisfying his own needs. This is not to be construed as meaning that the other is only an instrument to be used in the service of unrevealed purposes in the Machiavellian sense. Other people can become ends in themselves if we value them and provide support for their legitimate needs even as they serve our needs. Merely by recognizing that others have desires of their own which must be fulfilled in the cooperative process, we attach intrinsic rather than instrumental value to other people.

This form of cooperation requires that Socrates' famous aphorism "Know thyself" be extended. As we pointed out earlier, we know ourselves only as well as we know others. Similarly, in order to love ourselves we need to love others. We do not refer here to the egocentric narcissism described by Freud, which in fact denies that anyone else has intrinsic worth, nor to an ethic which would require that without reason we be our brother's keeper. "Love" as we use it here is an interpersonal transaction. In its deepest and most meaningful form, it is the unconditional acceptance of another by a person who has learned to know, to be aware of, and to accept himself. To "know thyself" and to "be your brother's keeper" imply the maintenance of individuality in a context of interpersonal communication. The ability to do so depends on a clear understanding of the processes of both learning and change, since personal growth is dependent on constructive and supportive relationships with others.

It is important to understand before we go on that *acceptance* of another person for what he is and what he stands for does not necessarily imply agreement with his views or methods. Acceptance of another person involves positive attitudes of respect, interest, caring, and trust, as well as the assumption of dependability, consistency, and the preservation of separateness based on an honest appraisal of differences. Self-acceptance is synonymous with self-awareness. Awareness, in turn, increases the capacity of individuals to attend to and respond to another individual or group. The degree to which this is possible can be measured by the extent to which an individual can respond meaningfully to a frame of reference other than his own. Thus, communication is inextricably bound to cooperation. "No man is an island," said the poet Donne, each is "a part of the main." Nowhere is this more true and more critical than in the life of the organization.

THE LEVELS OF PERSONAL INVOLVEMENT

Communication, which is the *sine qua non* of the cooperative process, may take place at several levels. There is what might be called the content level, that is, a transmission of information between persons, accompanied by no significant emotional involvement. A stranger steps up to another and asks street directions. Or the lecturer tells a group of interested students that certain animals hibernate with the coming of winter. Such exchanges concern matters that do no engage the feeling processes and therefore flow freely in response to universal needs for information.

A second level of communication could be described as one which involves interdependencies, such as those which occur between a superior and his subordinate. At this level, relational problems involving values or attitudes exist— as in the case of a superior discussing organizational goals—but they are minimized by the expectations each of those involved has about the attitudes and behavior of the other. If role differences are recognized and accepted and value differentials and rewards are consistent with these differences, communication and cooperation usually proceed without significant difficulty.

The deepest levels of communication are those which involve the relationship itself. In this case powerful emotions or feelings become factors. The outcome here may range from an exchange of understanding and cooperative behavior to an exchange of hostility, non-understanding, and aggression. In the former case, the self systems and pertinent values of those involved are compatible and mutually supportive. In the latter case, the failure to communicate is a result of the presence of threats to the self-system of one or the other or both persons involved.

In complex human communication the content, the prescribed interdependencies, and the nature of the relationship itself may all become involved simultaneously. When this occurs the flow of understanding between persons is an uncertain and complicated process. "Speech which goes from one to another between two natures, and, what is worse, between two experiences, is doubly relative." In these words, Robert Louis Stevenson captured the essence of the human communication problem. What is said by one person to another may reflect a conscious effort to distort true meanings or to cover up experiences which are perceived to be threatening. Distortions may occur for reasons which are not consciously known to the person involved. What is heard by the other person may likewise be filtered through a defensive screen which may or may not be adapting to reality. Hence, what is said may be only relative to that which cannot, without anxiety, be heard. In many cases, therefore, there may be little or no exchange of truth.

Fortunately, this state of affairs is not universal nor is it without remedy, as we shall see. The ability to communicate meaningfully is too important to the task of getting the world's work done. We speak to each other in order to understand each other, in order to coordinate our activities with those of others and, perhaps most important, in order to seek confirmation of ourselves through others. How can we improve this process? How are self-awareness and sensitivity to others related to communication and cooperation at the interpersonal level? Let us explore these matters further.

SOME NOTES FROM SYSTEMS THEORY

At a higher level of abstraction than interpersonal or interorganizational levels, cyberneticians think of all known phenomena as *systems phenomena.* Each system is controlled by an internal communication process and in turn is also related to other systems by external communication processes. Every system can be viewed as a system in its own right and simultaneously as a subsystem in a system of higher order which legitimizes the objectives and goals and more or less controls the destiny of the subsystem. Two persons conversing, for example, constitute a system which in varying degrees oversees and controls their behavior. In formal organizations prescribed statuses and positions both legitimize and control within wide or narrow limits the roles played by the persons occupying them.

All systems, including human systems, have inputs of various kinds which are used to enable the system to reach objectives—that is, to achieve certain qualities and quantities of output. Self-correcting mechanisms which control systems by furnishing them with information about the effects of system activity are referred to as *feedback loops*. If the self-correcting mechanism has a stabilizing influence on the system's output in relation to an objective or goal, it is said to be *negative feedback*. If, on the other hand, this mechanism *changes* the system output relative to the goal, it is called *positive feedback.* This internal communication network or feedback loop can be illustrated by referring to the operation of a home-heating system or voltage amplifier.

A thermostat as a servomechanism reads the mixture of hot and cold air in a room and compares the temperature reading to its own setting. If the surrounding temperature in the room is too low, the thermostat sends a message to the furnace to go on. The furnace responds by generating warm air which it conveys to the room where the thermostat is located. When sufficient warm air has been produced to increase the temperature to the set level, the thermostat returns information to the furnace indicating that its present output of warm air is no longer desired, i.e., sends a message which has the effect of shutting off the furnace. Thus, the thermostat-furnace system maintains equilibrium around the set temperature and controls action through information concerning the effect of the output of warm air. This information is continually transmitted, in fact, through a negative feedback loop.

Another example of the feedback concept, again from the physical world, is a voltage amplifying circuit.

A diagram of such a circuit is shown in Fig. 3. The input voltage A is amplified and appears as an increased or amplified signal, output voltage B. A part of the output is "fed back" to the input through the feedback circuit, represented by voltage C. The phase relationship or sign of this feedback voltage is such that it affects the amplitude and therefore the amount of distortion in the waveform, increasing it if "positive" and decreasing it if "negative."

Analogies to these physical systems can be drawn with respect to human systems. Karl Menninger in his book *The Vital Balance* describes how the healthy human body is able, despite constant irritations, to maintain a flexible balance internally among its parts as well as externally with the environment. He further describes how this concept applies to the human personality. If a person says, "I feel like I'm falling apart," he is expressing anxiety over a feeling that the essential unity and integrity of his personality is threatened. The ego's constant struggle to control the insistent demands of the id and the superego is an example

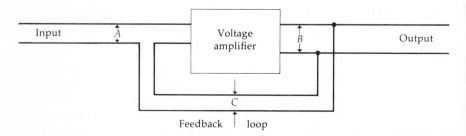

Fig. 3.   Voltage-amplifier feedback circuit.

of the principle of *homeostasis*—the attempt on the part of the human organism and its psychological and physiological processes to preserve a constant internal equilibrium in the face of external demands.

The concepts of negative feedback and homeostasis are adequate to describe the organism's attempts to maintain internal and external balance. However, they do not help us to explain the phenomenon of growth and change in the organism itself, under the influence of environmental forces. Homeostasis implies a return to a former state or a single basic goal. Yet, it is common knowledge that changes occur and that rather than being upsetting and regressive they can be improving and progressive. Learning new behaviors or unlearning old ones may contribute to an individual's competence. Indeed, without such growth there would be a relative decline in the individual's capacity to cope with new or threatening experiences. To put it another way, stability or equilibrium is a quality of "closed" systems, i.e., systems which are wholly or partially impervious to outside information and influence.

According to the concept of entropy, closed systems eventually degenerate, decay, and finally die because they exhaust available ordered energy necessary to perform work and are unable to draw new ordered energy from their environment. They are, therefore, unable to renew themselves. An "open" system, however, grows and changes in response to data and the infusion of new energy origination in the environment. If we believe that man seeks both accomplishment and understanding; i.e., self-actualization, we must also believe that he desires to move forward away from a steady state, away from simply "being," and toward "becoming." He must, therefore, be able to maximize his sensitivity or openness to the environment.

These concepts from systems theory can be applied not only to organic systems but to the processes of interpersonal communication. Just as in the case of the heating system and the voltage amplifier, the behavior of a person involved in interpersonal communication affects and is affected by the behavior of others. Given two persons in interaction, communication takes place as a mutual exchange of meanings in which feedback from one to the other and back again is constant and not always verbal.

THE INTERPERSONAL COMMUNICATION SYSTEM

In human communication, negative feedback functions to maintain equilibrium or stability, i.e., a continuation of existing interpersonal relationships. Positive feedback means change and may upset the system's equilibrium. This does not mean that negative feedback is "good" and positive feedback is "bad." Obviously, negative feedback would be "bad" if change were needed, "good" if a steady state or balance were required. Positive feedback would be "good" where deviation from present behavior is needed and "bad" where stability is the desired state. However, either type of feedback, in the absence of the other, can be destructive. Growth and development cannot occur in stable systems which are totally the product of continued negative feedback. On the other hand, positive feedback, which supports deviation from a given state or condition, could destroy the system if it continued uncontrolled. At some point, negative feedback (or reduction in deviation) must occur or the system would fly apart. In the same way, if positive feedback were to continue in the home heating system or the voltage amplifier beyond a critical point, serious temperature changes or oscillation could occur and the ultimate destruction of the system would be certain.

We need, therefore, to look more closely at the idea of positive feedback, which is associated with change, and its relationship to negative feedback in human communication. Change in individual man or in organizations results from learning new ways of thinking, new ways of responding, and new ways of behaving in relation to persons and events. Learning, however, is an internal matter controlled by the individual—by his intellectual capacity and his curiosity, as well as by the hindrances to learning imposed by his lack of self-acceptance as manifested in defensive behavior. Learning in interpersonal situations—pupil and teacher, player and coach, follower and leader—must, in order to be effective, be characterized by stability in the relationship and by a change in the pupil, player, or follower. There must exist, in other words, an interpersonal situation in which the learner can face the problem of change within acceptable limits of psychological stress. Too much positive feedback will upset the relationship; at some point along the way, negative feedback must be introduced in order to avoid this eventuality. Both types of feedback, therefore, are essential to learning but their relationship must be one of balance and complementarity.

In the context of interpersonal communication, negative feedback is information concerning how one's behavior affects others: "You seem angry with me." "Your idea about that seems very close to mine." Positive feedback is information concerning how one *should* or *ought* to behave. It establishes a new goal in the relationship toward which one or the other or both involved should strive. "Do it this way, not that way." "Try to think of a better way."

From these examples it is evident that communication not only conveys information about the object of the message but also about the subjects who are in communication. When personal levels of communication are involved, the information always contains sentiments and signs which define or attempt to define the *relationship* which exists between the persons, and some of the focus of attention shifts away from the content of communication to the selves of the participants. As this occurs, one person and then the other is, in effect, saying: "This is the way I seem to myself in relation to you, in this situation."

What occurs between one person's self and the other person's self, as the communication transaction unfolds, is some form and some degree of confirmation or disconfirmation of the other's sense of identity in that situation. Buber has said that in human society persons confirm one another to some extent or other, and a society is human in the measure to which its members do so. Not to confirm another's view of himself is to deny to that person his essential character and to attack the consistency of his self-concept or to indicate to him that he must change in some way if he is to be accepted by the other. *A great deal depends upon how and in what manner and in what circumstances disconfirmation occurs.*

Confirmation is a form of negative feedback or stabilizing influence as we saw in connection with the home heating system or the voltage amplifier examples. The person who receives confirmation about himself feels encouragement and is in harmony with himself, conditions which are conducive to an inner equilibrium and a sense of personal worth.

Person A says to person B: "Look at how well I am doing my work with this new equipment." This is both a statement concerning objects—the new equipment and the work—and a statement about A and his relationship to B. In effect, A is saying, "See what a clever person I am." because he feels a need to say it.

If person B directs his reply to the relational content of A's statement and says something like, "It is good work. You have done a good job," he confirms A's feelings of accomplishment and worth.

On the other hand, B's reply could be "That is an expensive machine. See that you treat it well." This response would contain a number of meanings which A might construe as derogatory or simply unrelated to what he was trying to get B to confirm about his, A's, self-feelings and evaluations. It could be diversionary, for one thing. To A it could mean that B, for some hidden and therefore unfriendly reason, wished to avoid A as a subject of discussion. It could be a *non sequitur*. To A it could be unrelated to what he had on his mind. It might also be a denial of A's concept of himself as a valuable contributor to a task perceived as mutually shared and toward which A believed himself to have some responsibility. Any or all of these meanings and others of a similar nature would seem threatening to A. They would indicate to A that some change in his behavior or in his attitudes was required. He could have feelings of guilt and anxiety. His responses to B might include a range of reactionary behaviors—defensiveness, i.e., frustration and withdrawal, resentment, and aggressiveness.

Person A could also respond by taking B's comment as reflecting a legitimate concern for the machine. This might lead him to take special care of it, i.e., change his implied behavior to accommodate B's wishes. In this case, however, his relationship with B would be one characterized by trust and openness where the need for self-confirmation had long since been recognized and given its appropriate place in their ongoing association. In other words, it would be a case in which B's behavior was matched by A's expectancies.

"BLACK BOX" INPUT-OUTPUT

In order to explore further the concepts of confirmation and disconfirmation, let us consider the thoughts and feelings of two individuals in communication and try to understand how instability or distortion develops in the communication process, and how self-awareness and sensitivity as manifested in feedback restore stability and contribute to interpersonal development.

For the purpose of discussion, let us assume that person L is learner and person T is teacher in a teaching-learning transaction at a level of involvement where feelings or "self" play a part. The situation is a training episode in which we want to effect changes in L's interpersonal behavior. These roles could also refer to those of subordinate and superior, pupil and coach, client and therapist, without essential differences in the manner in which they are acted out. They might also include two-way communication between peers who are engaged in a mutual exposure-feedback transaction, i.e., both persons, by exchanging information are alternately or simultaneously learning from and teaching the other in an "open" communication relationship.

The communication transaction between L and T as described above may be thought of as consisting of several parts or phases:

1) What L says,
2) What T thinks L said (or perceives L as saying),
3) What T says,
4) What L thinks T said, etc.

L and T, of course, are not merely responding to each other in terms of content; they are simultaneously influencing each other, on the basis of all sorts of internal directives, by means of "hidden" meanings, facial expressions, body postures, and other forms of actual and imputed feedback. Many of these meanings within meanings constitute or cause the distortion which enters the circuit through the psychological processes which are occurring in L and T as their communication transaction develops.

For purposes of analysis, let us break into the circuit at phase 1, "What L says," considering for the moment only its effect on T. Let us assume that T is an individual who has well-developed qualities of self-awareness (SA) and sensitivity (S). Under these circumstances it can be expected that T will be attentive to communications from L. Having a lower need to be defensive, T will display readiness for external sources of ideas, and a good capacity to respond to the situation around him. Because T's personality is more "open" than "closed," he will be able to attach a high degree of importance to messages from L, and will be inclined to look to L for contributions and ideas. Thus T will not suffer with over-concern for himself and under-concern for L. He will, therefore, have a balanced view of his self, both in relation to L and to mutual tasks at hand. These attitudes of T's will, in addition to increasing his span of attention, have the effect of reducing the amount of distortion in the circuit by reducing his tendency to ascribe meanings to L's words or gestures or both, based on imagined threats to self.

Moving now to phase 2, "What T thinks L said," we are concerned with T's *acceptance* of messages from L. In this phase, we focus on what T perceives L to be saying and on the operation of selective mechanisms in T which act to screen or filter L's message as it relates to T's needs and to his self-concept. Since T's SA and S factors are well developed, he will be conscious of the nature and effect of his "filtering mechanism" and be deeply concerned with L's point of view. He will transform the attentiveness of phase 1 into a two-way orientation and will avoid interpretations of what he hears L say, based on a unilateral application of personal standards and values. His entire attitude at this stage will be one of listening, of non-interference and non-evaluation of L as a person. Again, distortion in the circuit will be reduced because of T's ability to put himself more effectively into L's frame of reference—to see things as L does—and to make realistic use of what he hears and what he observes. Put another way, it will be easier for T to use the test of reality on what his ears tell him rather than the test of self-consciousness.

The third phase, "What T says," will be characterized by an absence in T of a need to attack either at the verbal level or in the form of offensive nonverbal feedback. Rather, his posture will be one of encouragement toward L, of non-dominance, nonthreat, and unconditional responsiveness. This is because T is willing to risk an encounter with feelings and even with negative messages from L. His responses will be expressions of interest, of curiosity, of willingness to "level" with L with appropriate rationality or feeling. He will be committed to the "here and now" interpersonal transaction which is taking place, free of facades and thus projecting a trusting relationship.

Before continuing, let us review for a moment some of the ideas which were discussed in the chapter on self and self-awareness. At the core of an individual's ideas of the way things "ought to be done" is his concept of self. Self is at the center of a system of values which the individual strives to maintain whole at all cost. Any attempt at invasion of this fortified system by what are perceived as disconfirming events—ones not good for the structure of self or its needs—will be resisted. Such resistance is a natural reaction and essential to the preservation of individuality. On the other hand, any action in the environment which is consistent with the person's value structure and self-concept; i.e., a confirming event, will be accepted and assimilated as being good and need-satisfying.

With these ideas in mind, let us look at the fourth phase of the communication circuit, "What L thinks T said." Because T is projecting attitudes which are perceived by L as expressing interest, a desire to be open, an acceptance of person, responsiveness, and sympathy, L experiences similar attitudes toward T. His feelings are those of an individual who is engaged in a confirming and deeply satisfying relationship. He has feelings of significance and worthiness, feelings of being wholly engaged in talking with T about the same things and at the same level of involvement. He is aware of an absence of masks and of deception and of repressed or unexpressed motivations. His interaction with T is genuine, warm, and deeply human. Defensiveness is minimized and, in fact, at conscious levels may be totally absent. In his responses, therefore, L is leveling with T in the same way that T is leveling with L in an open, meaningful, and productive human relationship. Let us now review the incident set forth at the beginning of this chapter. A draftsman, in revolt over a heavy workload and deadline, has just asked the supervisor, "What's going on here, Frank?" This remark, as we pointed out, contains a number of communicational elements. It includes factual information or content. He has received some sketches from engineers to translate into drawings. It also includes emotional coloring which appears to concern not only his cooperative interdependencies with the engineering group, but also interdependencies between him and Frank. Finally, it concerns the quality of his and Frank's personal relationship. As we noted earlier, these are the ingredients of a complex communication problem. Both the flow of understanding as well as voluntary cooperation can be preserved or easily jeopardized, depending upon Frank's response.

Frank might fall into the fateful trap of believing that the draftsman, being a rational person, will share Frank's assessment of the situation and respond accordingly. Let us assume that Frank sees deadlines, production levels, and the need to cooperate with the engineers. From this frame of reference, he might say, "Well, let's get off the dime," or words to this effect. However, the draftsman, having his own set of needs, perceptions, and motives, may not share his boss's view of the situation. He undoubtedly feels that he is being harrassed unfairly by the engineers, and may now feel that Frank has joined them in unreasonable expectations. Frank's response will, in this case, come through to him as destructive positive feedback, his cooperation will be reluctant, his feelings will be turned inward to feed upon his frustration. His relationship with Frank, if even only slightly, must deteriorate.

On the other hand, Frank might try to address himself to the problem as the draftsman saw it, or at least admit to himself that the draftsman could have a point which was at yet unclear. With this attitude he might reply quite differently, "You feel like it's too much to ask." No jumping to conclusions. No evaluation. No implied denial of the draftsman's credibility and worth. In this case, Frank's attitude is supportive and confirming. It *encourages* a rational rather than a frustrated response. If the draftsman's anti-engineers feeling is strong, he may, of course, elaborate on his feelings. The incident could become a springboard for more trouble for Frank. However, this approach could set the stage for a truly therapeutic relationship. Since Frank has interjected a negative feedback nonevaluative impulse into their interpersonal communication system at the right moment, equilibrium has been maintained. The draftsman, instead of being forced further into his frustration, may now more easily accept a balanced view of the situation and be more problem-solving and helpful, reciprocating Frank's supportiveness, and see that Frank has a problem too. Perhaps he will voluntarily revise his own hostile attitude toward the engineering group. Of such delicacy and finesse is the stuff of human communication!

In contrast to this, there are times when feelings between two individuals completely block communication. A situation of this kind could be termed a *confrontation*. When this occurs gaps appear in the communication circuit between phases 1 and 2, and between phases 3 and 4. The individuals involved act as though their attitudes have polarized, each one believing that he is right, the other wrong; that he is good, the other bad. A win-lose conflict tends to develop. The clash generates negative feelings which are further aggravated by evaluative feedback which neither party finds acceptable and which increases defensive attitudes as each participant strives to preserve his position (and self-image) in the face of a threatening, disconfirming, experience. Evidences of low mutual consideration may be accompanied by a strong desire on the part of each individual to achieve and maintain control over the other. When confrontation occurs between individuals, little or no consistent and meaningful exchange of ideas can take place unless 'the gaps in their communication circuit can be closed.

The following case illustrates the problems which may occur in a confrontation between two individuals.

Mrs. Helen Grover, about fifty years of age, came to work as a clerk at the library of Trenton College in December. The recently completed accreditation study had recommended that the librarian be assigned a full-time clerk because she was greatly overloaded with work.

During the first week of work, Mrs. Grover was highly nervous. When given a job such as making typewritten duplicates of catalog cards, she brought each item of the job back to Miss Hewitt, the librarian, for verification as she completed it. She engaged the librarian in long conversations about the reasons for such procedures and argued about the spelling of words in titles, attempting to justify her ideas of how the words should be spelled.

She made a great number of complaints during the first six weeks about her working conditions: the light struck her in the eyes the wrong way (her desk was moved); the chair was too low (a pillow was provided); her typewriter skipped (the repair man could find no defect); the ribbon was too light (she was given a dark one); the air was impure (she sprayed constantly because of her allergies); the dark typewriter ribbon caused smudges on the paper (she was given a large eraser).

A month after Mrs. Grover's arrival, Miss Hewitt decided that a heart-to-heart talk was indicated. She mentioned such items to Mrs. Grover as the continual arguments about details, and the time taken from Miss Hewitt's own work. Mrs. Grover wept copiously, saying that she was happy in her job and that she didn't realize she was not doing her work well. She promised to do better. She did work quietly for about a week. Then she reverted to her usual chatter.

In our traditional ways of looking at interpersonal problems, this case would probably be dismissed as simply a personality clash between two incompatible individuals or, worse, with the conviction that Mrs. Grover was "some kind of nut." Miss Hewitt seems clearly to have reached this latter conclusion after some arm's-length attempts to respond to a series of incidents which are symptomatic that a problem exists. She now views Mrs. Grover as the *locus* of the problem and has neglected to explore with her possible external sources of difficulty such as the demands of the new job, new working relationships, or other organizational problems. Since, as we have emphasized, the behavior of people is a product of both personality and situation, Miss Hewitt by not keeping this clearly before her has set the stage for a serious breakdown in communication between herself and Mrs. Grover, and may have deprived herself of a source of information about problems in the library organization which need her attention. Less action based on Miss Hewitt's view of the situation and more listening to Mrs. Grover might have brought these out at an earlier point in the sequence of events and at less cost to the organization. Instead, Miss Hewitt has laid the groundwork for a possible confrontation between herself and Mrs. Grover, which may result in the latter's dismissal or voluntary departure. If Mrs. Grover is *not* the problem as

Miss Herwitt has assumed and Miss Herwitt continues her "one-way" approach to communication with future replacements for Mrs. Grover, one must wonder whether the recommendation made in the accreditation study that Miss Hewitt be "assigned a full time clerk because she was greatly overloaded with work" will ever come to fruition.

Following is a case in which confrontation has fully developed.

In the pediatrics section of Metropolitan Hospital, a volunteer "play lady," Miss Ann, made it a practice to read to some of the children during play periods. Mrs. Andrews, the hospital librarian, became upset about this and told Miss Ann on several occasions that she wasn't to do this, that this was the librarian's job. Considerable ill-feeling developed between the two women over this, so much so that Mrs. Andrews decided to talk over the situation with Miss Bolton, supervisor of the pediatric nursing service, and made an appointment for this purpose.

Mrs. Andrews was visibly disturbed when she arrived in Miss Bolton's office. "Miss Bolton, I felt I just had to talk with you. Miss Ann is making me feel so uncomfortable. She is so sarcastic and contradicts everything I say. I try to decide what stories the children should be reading, and you know the rheumatic fever patients shouldn't be reading anything exciting. If she's going to bring the older children to the library in the afternoon, I don't think she should act as if I don't know what I'm doing when I suggest books. After all, I have had years of library training and specialized in bibliotherapy, and I don't think anyone should ever give out a book to any patient unless she has read it herself. I've read every book in the patient's library, and I know just exactly what is in each book I give out to every patient. And Ann has just been insolent to me. I never had any trouble with the girl who was play lady just before her."

"Well, Mrs. Andrews, I am surprised to hear you say this about Ann. She never appeared to be impolite. I think perhaps. . . . "

"Well, she is. And she is so irresponsible with our phonograph records that I told her I didn't want her borrowing them anymore. I found an album I gave her last week on the private division today."

"Miss Ann explained that to me. She sent one of the older girls back with it before closing time, and Judy left it on the library desk because no one was there. Ann said she felt she should have taken it back herself and would next time."

"I don't want her using them again or reading to the children. You know I visit every patient in the hospital every day and read to anyone who wants me to. I even come back after supper if my work isn't done. I have a call number, and the operator can call me any time someone wants a book. You know bibliotherapy is very important in helping a patient get well."

"Now, Mrs. Andrews, I appreciate all you are willing to do for the patients, but I also feel that Dr. King and I have direct responsibility for the care of the children when they are in the hospital. Miss Ann is responsible to me, and I feel that if Dr. King and I agree on her duties, then it it up to us to determine what she shall be permitted to do. Our nurses and student volunteers have had instruction in child growth and development, and reading to the youngsters is one of the best ways we have to develop comfortable, happy relationships with them."

"I don't think nurses are bibliotherapists. And Dr. King is satisfied with what I'm doing. He has never said that he wasn't. The doctors on the other services think I do a good job, too."

"I'm sorry, Mrs. Andrews, that we have been having all this trouble. I think perhaps we had better try to have a meeting with Dr. King and see if we can't define one another's responsibilities a little more completely. I'm sorry, but I have a meeting with the new medical student class now. I'll be getting in touch with you again soon."

The confrontation here between two polarized points of view is so nearly complete that little, if any, meaning has been exchanged between the two women. To use Carl Rogers' colorful description, all we have here is " . . . just two ideas, two feelings, two judgments missing each other in psychological space." Miss Bolton has one point of view, Mrs. Andrews another. Miss Bolton, in her eyes, is right, Mrs. Andrews wrong. Each perceives the other as threatening, negative, and disconfirming, and each is striving to gain control of the other on her own terms. The very real conflicts between Miss Ann and Mrs. Andrews and now between Miss Bolton and Mrs. Andrews were swallowed up in the power play called by the nursing service supervisor. In the aftermath, Mrs. Andrews resigned from the hospital and the confrontation was never resolved. In Miss Bolton's eyes, the "villain" had been uncovered and the librarian's departure was the occasion for relief. The forces which created Miss Bolton's villain, however, remained obscured behind a curtain of misunderstandings, accusations, and feelings which could only have been drawn aside through communicative skills which all too often are unknown to those in positions of leadership in our organizational society.

In summary, then, interpersonal communication is a reciprocal, mutually reinforcing process which has as its aim an exchange of understandings between two people at the deepest personal levels. Where feelings are involved, the problem of understanding is a creation of the relationship itself. The focus of the whole process is turned inward on the complex defense systems and self-concepts of each person involved. Since each is impelled by basic forces to maintain self-consistency, each can make this task easier for the other through his self-awareness and sensitivity. In this way each can usher into the relationship an openess and security which can add new dimensions to the interpersonal process of exchanging meanings and ideas.

Cooperation sometimes requires change in interpersonal behavior. An individual's competence, as a leader, to facilitate constructive change in others, or his capacity to *accept* necessary changes in his own attitudes and behavior, as a *prelude* to leadership, requires special training. Such procedures involve the practicing, or in the absence of necessary ability, the acquiring of knowledge and skills in interpersonal relations involving change. Where personal change is concerned, the individual must recognize the need for change and his training must emphasize that he has the power to re-educate himself. "If you want to improve, you have it within yourself to do so" is a basic tenet of all person-centered change procedures. These procedures, which are closely related to the communication process, will be explained in the next chapter.

CHAPTER EIGHT

ALTERING THE SELF

". . . . The motivation for learning and change springs from the self-actualizing tendency of life itself. . . ."

CARL ROGERS

In an earlier chapter we said that man's nature is not a *given* that exists indepen-dently of experience, but rather is a product of experience. Man's understanding of man is to be found in his system of needs and attitudes, reflecting his personal history. People are what we have learned to believe they are, what we expect them to be. What we assume about others conditions our behavior toward them and their behavior toward us. Our effectiveness in interpersonal relationships is re-flected in our attitudes which others sense or perceive and to which they respond. In the traditional bureaucratic culture, based on a hierarchy of organizational authority and chain of command, there exists, we believe, a generally pessimistic view of human nature. If we would deal with the consequences of this view—the discouragement of spontaneous and internally derived motives and ideas concerning work—we must consider how traditional attitudes can be changed in the leadership of organizations. This requires that we consider the self or the self-concept to explore ways and means which are potentially useful for altering attitudes.

ACTIVE LEARNING

There are essentially two basic ways of altering an individual's social behavior. One way is to help him reorganize his internal patterns of feelings and attitudes toward himself and toward others. The other way is to train, teach or educate him in an effort to remedy specific inadequacies. The former method builds upon the internal capacities and capabilities of the person being changed, while the latter is concerned with rectifying a real or assumed lack of knowledge. Changing an individual's social behavior by seeking to improve his skill in dealing with others is a complex process. A prerequisite may be that he acquire new knowledge and obtain new understanding both from and about the external world. Often, bringing about change means that the individual must unlearn or modify certain attitudes he has about others and about himself. A final condition is that he learn to use other things he has learned in his life experience more effectively.

Social learning based upon intensive interaction between the learner and teacher, a process which draws upon personal initiative and involvement, produces more lasting and more effective results than learning acquired through passive absorption of knowledge. Studies show that learning is facilitated if the learner himself takes, or is given, an active part in the process—even if his activity consists merely of clenching and unclenching his fist while engaged in listening to a lecture! When he becomes genuinely ego-involved in the process, the favorable results are intensified. In a classic study, Kurt Lewin demonstrated that women in a group who discussed together the need during wartime to use more of the poorer cuts of meat were much more likely to do so than those who merely heard an interesting lecture about it. He concluded that passive listening without a direct supportive interpersonal relationship and personal activity on the part of the learner is conducive to psychological isolation, a condition in which individual recognition and social acceptance are minimal, and in which, as a consequence, little incentive exists for absorbing new ideas.

THE CHANGER-CHANGEE RELATIONSHIP

What we are saying, then, is that the learner or changee must take an active part in changing himself, i.e., initiate change from within. This statement is based on the concept, borrowed from psychotherapy, that if attitude and behavior changes suggested by the learning process are not perceived as meaningful and true, the subject will not alter his self-perception, and no change in his self-concept will occur. This theory places the *source* of change in the learner or changee, but it does not mean that the teacher or change agent plays a passive role. On the contrary, his skill and empathy are indispensable elements in the change process.

Change from within requires a special kind of relationship between the change agent and the changee. First of all, the change agent must assume that the individual, given the opportunity, has within himself positive forces for change. Thus the change agent can be more concerned with understanding the changee's point of view and less concerned with evaluating what the changee is saying or doing. The changee's frame of reference, including his needs and feelings, assumes greater importance than the change agent's, a situation which is at variance with many of our traditional ideas about the status relationship between student and teacher. Teacher-centered training may, at times, be more suitable for imparting intellectual content, but it is of less value when the object is change in a person's attitudes or behavior. The impetus for change and the capacity for understanding his own feelings and perceptions are found in the changee and may be understood only dimly, if at all, by the change agent. The same may be said of any behavioral change relationship whether it involves the manager and managed, the coach and his team members, mother and child, therapist and client, or the dynamics of change in group life.

A change in attitudes and related behavior requires an evaluation by the changee of self. This is not possible in the absence of a "safe" psychological climate in which to make such an evaluation. Research has shown that empathy on the part of the change agent is essential. His ability to project his own consciousness warmly and imaginatively, accompanied by a perception of warmth and acceptance by the other person, facilitates self-evaluation by the changee and supports his motive to change. When empathy is absent in the change relationship, resistance to change increases.

This concept of change is based on optimistic assumptions concerning the nature of man and a consciousness or awareness of self as a separate and unique entity moving through a continuum of experience which stretches from birth to death. It recognizes that existence is purely personal and only the individual can differentiate from the field of his experience those elements which are consistent with and supportive of his self. If there are in this field objects or forces which seem to threaten the integrity of the self system, the mechanisms of defense block out their effect unless the individual's need to know is so strong that it prevails and to some extent overcomes such mechanisms.

The need to know is, therefore, a powerful agent for change. But it cannot have effect unless the changee becomes aware of the flaws in his self-structure which prevent him from further personal growth. He must, in other words, find it possible to look critically at himself. The function of the change agent, therefore, is to maintain a supportive climate that will minimize for the changee the defensive forces which would prevent a re-examination of weaknesses in the self structure. The change agent thus does not act directly but indirectly in effecting change; he merely helps to make it possible for the changee to alter his own perceptions and sometimes serves as a model, meeting the needs of the changee for new forms of behavior to replace the old.

This relationship between a change agent and the changee is to be found in holistic systems of psychotherapy such as those of Carl Rogers and Karen Horney. These therapists emphasize the unity of the individual and man's capacity for finding his own way toward creative solutions to his behavioral problems. Therapeutic systems, however, are a product of and are directed toward problems and solutions relating to mental illness and the neuroses. Our concern in this book is with change processes which are *related* to these systems but which are *training*-oriented, i.e., have as their purpose helping "normal" people to realize and develop latent potentials for better interpersonal relationships through increased awareness, self-acceptance, and the re-shaping or reforming of attitudes.

THE CHANGE PROCESS

Change, that is in the sense of one person changing another, is often discussed in a moral or ethical context involving ends and means. Frequently authors argue that it is unethical or immoral for one person to change another because change becomes an exercise in manipulation. The one who is changed is pictured as the victim of a crafty and superior intellect who, for often unspecified purposes of his own, manages or controls the thought and behavior of the other. It cannot be denied that interpersonal behavior at this level is frequent in our economic society.

Bringing about change is not meant here in this manipulative sense. Manipulation by one person of another is change from without. That is, the forces for change, including the motives and therefore the purposes, are in the change agent. They are external to the one who is to be changed. Change as we discuss it here involves voluntary change from within. The purpose is to improve the capacity of the changee to handle interpersonal relationships, to make him more effective as a person. The purpose is not to make him a better instrument of society or of the organization, although these consequences may, of course, be by-products of the change process.

The difference between change from within and change from without may be viewed as slight, but we feel that it has great significance in the change relationship. Since it is our view that growth and development along personal dimensions represent a universal need of mankind, defining change as self-improvement is a natural corollary. Change from within requires that the change agent enter into a helping relationship with others. Such a helping relationship aims at providing the conditions whereby another person, in terms of his own motivations and his own purposes, accepts responsibility for finding his way toward becoming a more effective member of the organization and of society. The change agent thus becomes the instrument of the changee and assumes a facilitating rather than a controlling role.

The difference between facilitation and control can perhaps be illustrated by the following example.

The commanding officer of a U.S. Naval vessel found that he was having trouble with gambling aboard his ship. In the days following payday, each crew compartment had its own game going, and he knew that some of the men were heavy losers. He was puzzled as to how to handle this problem. He discussed it with his executive officer, and several lines of thought emerged. He could remind the men of a naval regulation against gambling on board ship and establish a roving patrol of masters-at-arms with orders to place violators under arrest. He could ignore the situation. Or he could quietly pass the word around among his senior petty officers that he was concerned about the consequences of gambling aboard his ship and would like to see them reduce it, if not stop it altogether. He knew from an earlier experience that any attempt at control through the master-at-arms force would simply drive the practice underground. Happily, he chose the alternative of involving the petty officers in the project. They suggested to him that he set up a "banking plan" in which the disbursing officer would be asked to limit the amount of cash in circulation by holding payroll money on the books during cruises while at the same time encouraging the men to make out allotments to families and banks ashore. These allotted funds would be automatically dispatched, as directed by the individual crew member, by the Navy's central disbursing office—a procedure which was already a part of established policy.

If the captain had chosen the way of *force* he would have used his master-at-arms detail. He chose, however, to *facilitate* the elimination of gambling by getting the support and carrying out the suggestion of the senior petty officers in the crew. It worked like a charm and created immense goodwill between the enlisted personnel and the ship's command.

To one whose sensitivity to the capacities of others is blocked by a lack of trust or a need to dominate, change is seen as a function of external forces which he as a change agent controls. He assumes, therefore, that altering another person's behavior requires the application of power to force the changee to respond in a predictable way. The assumption is that such an approach enables the change agent to retain control of the changee and to make better predictions concerning his future behavior. The changee literally is given no choice but to respond to the wishes of the change agent. The nature of the external sources of power used by the change agent who adopts this point of view depends on the change agent's own value and motivational system and may consist of physical coercion, rules of law and procedure, a superior intellect, sanctions of various kinds, and other forces based outside the changee.

This kind of change process is characteristic of a robot-view of human nature. Its implications are essentially negative. The changee responds out of a desire to lessen his pain—mental or physiological—rather than increase his pleasure. As a consequence, he adopts the practical view that a limited giving of himself is all that is necessary, and he performs only those acts which meet the change agent's minimum of acceptability. Like a robot he is deprived of spontaneity and originality. No one who has taught school can fail to have observed these effects and the deadening conformity produced by a grading system, for example, whose purpose has deteriorated to that of measuring the extent to which students parrot back what the teacher wants to hear.

Change based upon a helping relationship is an entirely different process. In contrast to the master-slave situation implicit in the robot theory, or change from without, the *empathic change process* is based upon a relationship in which the change agent is the means, not the changee. This kind of relationship is closer to a pilot view of man, i.e., it assumes that the changee is capable of taking the responsibility for learning and has the capacity to think and make acceptable choices. Under the robot concept there is no learning in the sense of personal growth, development, and initiation of action; there is only *knowing* and *reaction*. Behavioral change may take place but only to avoid punishment. Emphasis is on the avoidance of *not* doing rather than on doing well. True learning on the other hand, involves a growing and a developing from within the changee which, under the proper circumstances, results in the adoption and acting out of new patterns of behavior.

DEFINITION OF TRAINING

Traditional use of the term training refers to the activities in an organization whereby a new member is introduced to the rules which will govern him. Through orientation, indoctrination, and instruction he is trained to become an effective member of the organization. Training in this sense serves to perpetuate the existing order and values of the organization.

Our use of *training* refers to efforts at introducing a change in the attitudes and values of a member of the organization. Self-awareness, as we have seen, is the key to an opening of self to a wider range of experience. An increase in self-awareness leads to a reduction in defensive behavior, to expanded feelings of personal unity and consistency. It also enhances the meaningfulness and hence the efficiency of interpersonal relationships. *Opening of self to experience* implies the capacity to be aware of self-satisfying and self-ennobling encounters with the environment (particularly interpersonal encounters). In addition, it implies the capacity to recognize and accept experiences which seem to be *self-confirming* whether they are positive *or* negative in nature. They all contribute to our concept of being integrated. Even negative experiences, those in which we do not measure up to our self-concept, may be accepted as a natural part of our existence if similar experiences have been incorporated into our awareness at some more favorable time. As we have pointed out, self-awareness and self-acceptance are synonymous. Both are basic to the growth of the individual in the direction of making him become more aware of and sensitive to others. Accepting the presence of good and bad in oneself makes it easier to see that others may also be good and bad, and that it is the totality of the self, an integrated expression of one's personality, that is important.

Self-awareness was earlier defined as the proportion of the self of which we are conscious or that which is known to us. It represents what we are aware of, the sum total of the thought processes and feelings which define the conscious, personal self. The other portion of the personal self consists of the experiences we have denied because we perceived them as inconsistent with the self. If the two parts of the internal self structure, the conscious and the unconscious, could be conceived of as finite, an index of self-awareness could then be described quantitatively as the ratio between them, having theoretical limits which approach zero in the case of closed self systems and infinity in open self systems. In other words, as the conscious increases relative to the unconscious, the index of self-awareness increases, and vice-versa.

It follows, therefore, that if we are to increase the extent of our openness to experience, i.e., increase our index of self-awareness, we must increase the inputs from experience which we are able to accept as being consistent with our self. We must go through a process of change that alters our self system by reducing its unconscious defenses and increasing our contact with reality. Since the self system is a product of social experience, it may be altered by social experiences that enable the individual to re-examine and re-evalute his capacity to cope with situations which seem to involve threats to his self.

Under the influence of hereditary, environmental, and subjective forces, our self system constantly changes throughout life. In this process, conflict is ever present between one's self-concept, one's biology, and the environment. We resolve these conflicts either through adapting their sources to an existing concept of self or through changes in the self system which involve the incorporation of new ideas accompanied by corresponding alterations in the self-structure. As a whole, this process of adjustment and adaptation should be positive and growth-producing. Too often, however, even "normal" people are overwhelmed by the imperfections of past experience or by existing social norms and values. The process of personal growth which would contribute to the creation of a better interpersonal world becomes hampered by defensive behavior. Or the very underlying consistency of the self is accompanied by inertia, and thus the rate of change in the self structure is too slow to meet the necessities of effective behavior in particular situations. In these cases, the process of change must be given new directions or it must be accelerated.

With these thoughts in mind, let us consider now some of the training methods which are designed to increase our index of self-awareness. Following a brief introductory description of each of the principal methods, we will discuss similarities and differences in the learning processes involved, the nature of the subject matter and levels of personal involvement, and the outcomes or results which may be expected from each method.

THE CASE METHOD

One of the oldest and still widely used forms of training is the case method. When we refer to human relations cases we are reminded of "cases" used in other areas of study and research. For example, in the judicial process, the judge will make reference to the case on the docket. In this particular instance, the term "case" refers to a complete description of the situation on which there is a dispute. In addition, the case will also be built upon by the evidence introduced by the attorneys appearing before the court. A record will be added of the decisions made in similar cases, for the purpose of showing precedence and to encourage the judge to be consistent with relevant decisions made in the past. As the case goes on, it may assume a magnitude which makes it humanly impossible for the judge or members of the jury to read every single page of evidence and testimony. The judicial procedures, therefore, continually flush to the surface a condensation or a digest of the most important factors to be taken into account. Finally, the judge renders his decision based upon the data that, in his mind, have become strategically important.

In the field of medicine we also find references to "cases", but here the cases refer to individuals. A case history includes a detailed account of all pertinent material in the individual's background as well as an exploration of all the symptoms which characterize his illness. Included also are quantities of technical data from laboratory tests, X-rays, and other testing procedures. The critical task is up to the physicians who must read and interpret the data, reach a diagnosis of the patient's illness, and prescribe treatment. Thus we see that in the case in legal practice, there may be too much data and yet an absence of the critical data or the conclusive evidence. Similarly, in medical practice the physician may have an abundance of data only some of which may be relevant; perhaps the most critical data are not available because they cannot be uncovered without surgical intervention.

The human relations case combines some of the attributes of both legal and medical cases. It is a record of data obtained through research, observation, and measurement concerning an organizational situation. The problem, if there indeed is one, is solved by trainees through an analysis and discussion of its nature, the causes, and the various possible solutions. The solution which seems to have the best promise of success must then be selected.

In the case discussion, perhaps the most important phase of the human relations case, each trainee's input is accepted as valid. The discussion, therefore, provides a vehicle for the display of different values and attitudes, and a review of these in relation to identification with the characters in the case. This review may, at a safe level, encourage personal review of private values and attitudes as they emerge in the social context of the case and its discussion.

ROLE-PLAYING

As we grow into adulthood and assume responsibilities in a variety of social contexts, we are required to play many different roles or parts. We learn our various roles in interaction with others, e.g., parents, playmates, teachers, peers, superiors, and subordinates. The way we play our roles is determined in part by subjective forces—our feelings toward others, our evaluations of their feelings about us, and the way these evaluations affect our self-concept. It is also determined by those objective societal standards we recognize and in terms of our perception of these standards. Hence, we learn role behavior from a complex variety of interdependent sources.

We have one view, the subjective view, concerning our concept of rights, obligations, and duties of particular roles. This may or may not coincide with the objective view, the way other people expect to see a role-player behave. Sometimes we have opportunities to discuss these differences and thus learn something about ourselves which will encourage us to institute changes in our role-playing behavior. A superior who understands the communication process and the role of the self-concept in interpersonal relations can often act as "coach" in such instances. Most of the time, however, we do not have such opportunities, or the psychological atmosphere of the moment may not be right for such discussions. Role-playing as a training device helps us to overcome these problems, first, by providing us with opportunities to try out a role and to experiment with different role behaviors and, second, by providing a setting in which discussion may take place without damage to our self-concept.

In a role-playing training session we may be presented with partially structured situations—disciplining a subordinate, discussing with the boss our failure to get a promotion, and others—in which we play "ourselves." After the role-play, the leader of the group encourages us and the others who are learners to take an analytical look at our role behavior. Because we have the opportunity to practice without penalty and because the psychological atmosphere is purposely made to be as nonthreatening as possible, we are free to go through with a self-analysis and to hear the impressions of others. We learn to become more aware of ourselves in situations involving interpersonal relations, and we can practice more effective behavior.

At the same time, as we become more aware of our repertoire of behavior, we have the opportunity to exchange roles with others and to see their roles as they see them. In effect, we are able, partially, to assume their frame of reference and gain insights into features of their behavior which may not have been apparent to us before. Thus, role-playing as a training process increases our self-awareness and our sensitivity toward others in a variety of social situations.

LABORATORY TRAINING

This method of training is an omnibus for many training modes or styles. Like the case method and role-playing, laboratory training may include traditional methods such as lectures, reading, studying, and theoretical discussion. However, these methods are used only when they contribute to an understanding of the "here and now," a term which will be explained shortly. Laboratory training also incorporates the case method and role-playing if the occasion warrants doing so.

Perhaps the most distinguishing feature of the laboratory method lies in the sensitivity training or T-group (training group) approach to personal and organizational change. The T-group method is based on the theory that learning about oneself, others, and groups is facilitated when people individually and in groups are placed in situations where their own "here and now" behavior is analyzed and discussed. Persons in groups in a training laboratory usually start out in an unstructured setting where the accepted purpose or goal and, indeed, the only thing there is to do, is to talk about each other in the struggle with problems of identity, intimacy, personal and group goals, authority, inclusion and exclusion, and other deeply personal and often threatening problems. Every effort is made by those in charge of the laboratory, the "trainers," to eliminate stereotyped settings and cultural props, to encourage experimentation, and to assist participants in the often socially taboo processes of exposing themselves and giving and receiving feedback. Once this "here and now" climate of the laboratory has been established, the case method and role-playing are also sometimes used when the groups are concerned with particular types of problems.

As an example of a T-group, let us look at a brief excerpt from the beginning of a training session. About ten people are sitting in a circle in a room set aside for this purpose. They may be sitting in chairs or they may be disposed Indian-fashion or lounging on the floor. Here is a transcript of the early minutes of their discussion.

A: *I guess we're supposed to talk about ourselves. They don't seem to want us to do anything special.*

B: *Yeah. They didn't give us much to go on.*
[*Several moments of silence*]

C: *Why don't we start by introducing ourselves—telling each other something about ourselves?*

D: *I don't think they'd like that. They aren't interested in who we were, are they? . . . Or who we are?*
[*Laughs nervously*]

E: *I agree. Let's not go into that.*

C: *I think we need to know something about a guy so when he says something it will have a context. Know what I mean?*
[*More moments of silence*]

F: *Come on, M (the trainer), tell us what we're supposed to do!*
M: *You're doing fine.*
C: *Fine, he says! What is that supposed to mean?*
  ⌈*A and D both start talking at once*⌉
B: *I think we need a chairman.*

This brief illustration of the beginning of a T-group session reveals the difficulties that arise as the members begin the attempt to make sense of their predicament. Basic individual and group problems have already appeared in the discussion. There are symptoms of frustration and anxiety as the ambiguity of the situation is brought into focus. The group is trying to establish a goal and some rules for controlling the behavior of its members. It is seeking to structure their relationships (asking for a chairman). C is concerned with the problem of identity. Who am I? Where do I fit here? The uncertainty of his status and role, perhaps more clearly and comfortably defined at home, may be causing him anxiety. C and D seem engaged in a struggle for control. Who's in charge here? C wants one thing, D another. E sides with D. F is also concerned with who is in charge and where the locus of power is, as he calls for help from their "expert" or "leader." These and other problems are beginning to emerge and, as in real life, some of them will eventually create stubborn blockages as the group moves toward whatever goal it accepts. In real life there are barriers which prevent us from dealing directly and realistically with these very real symptoms of emotions and their obstructive influence on group progress. In the T-group an effort is made to weigh the functions and dysfunctions of such barriers through experimentation. There is also a conscious willingness to level with one another, and a desire to understand better and to cope with the problems of interpersonal, intragroup, and intergroup life.

Laboratory training is distinguished from group therapy, such as is used in mental clinics and hospitals, by the fact that it is oriented toward human relations training rather than toward the adjustment or elimination of abnormal behavior. In group therapy the purpose is to explore the reasons underlying some individual mental problem in an effort to establish a base from which an improvement by all may be made. Human relations training is aimed at developing and improving social skills and normal interpersonal relationships. Thus, though the methods and assumptions of group therapy and laboratory training are often similar, the purposes and the clientele are quite different.

THE LEARNING PROCESS

The underlying conceptual framework of the case method (as it is here conceived), of role-playing, and of laboratory training is the same. This framework involves certain assumptions concerning the nature of man, the role of the participant, the role of the change agent (teacher or trainer), and the learning process. The role of the participant is active rather than passive. He is explicitly recognized as capable of making choices. These choices will, in fact, accurately reflect his needs in relation to change as he is experiencing the need to change. The primary role of the teacher or trainer is to encourage conditions in which the need for defensive behavior is minimized and the individual's capacity to respond constructively to both internal and external influences can be explored and evaluated. The trainer role must, therefore, be supportive and provide the participants with maximum freedom to consider alternatives and make decisions.

The learning cycle or process under these various training methods in essentially the same, consisting of

1) the discovery of an inadequacy,
2) the presence of a change agent,
3) the absence of threat to the existing self-structure and the reduction of self-defense,
4) self-insight,
5) the discovery of new attitudes,
6) incorporation of these attitudes into the self-structure, and
7) an increase in the readiness of the self system to receive inputs from experience.

The discovery of an inadequacy is accompanied by feelings of anxiety. Let us suppose, for example, that the group has attributed certain values to an individual in a group problem-solving situation. These values are condemned by the group as detrimental to achieving the group's goal of solving the problem. The individual is thus suddenly confronted with the possibility of failure, a failure to live up to his own expectations and a failure to be the kind of person he thinks others expect him to be. His sense of security is jeopardized, his confidence is weakened. He may try to escape, to fight, to rationalize, to locate the cause of his difficulty in another person or in the group. However, he may, under appropriate conditions, face up to himself and try to re-examine attitudes of which he has been unaware or only dimly aware but which may be the cause of his difficulty.

So we see that if our anxiety occurs in a supportive, helping atmosphere in which norms relating to experimentation and interpersonal authenticity have been made explicit and are accepted, conditions are present which have the power to reduce our defenses and make a re-examination of our self possible. Under these conditions, we do not feel under attack for our failure. Rather, we are aware of a feeling that others are trying to understand our anxieties and help us overcome them. We can construe their feedback concerning our failures as helpful rather than punitive, especially where, under the trainer's guidance, such feedback is given in descriptive rather than evaluative terms. We feel free to re-evaluate, to review, and perhaps to achieve a moment of profound and significant self-insight. The creation of this kind of atmosphere is the first and most important responsibility of the change agent whether he is involved in the case method, a role-playing situation, or laboratory training.

Not feeling threatened and having decided to alter particular attitudes, we seek new ones. We may find them in the group or in the change agent. Or the moment of self-insight may be so deep and searching that we discover new ways of thinking about the situation within our own thought processes, in our reason itself. These ideas, which now seem to us to be more appropriate than those which led to our rejected behavior are taken over, incorporated, and become a part of self-organization. The structure of self thus is altered and a new integration advances from the old. Attitudes which had previously distorted the kind of experience which led to our disconfirmation by the group and to the accompanying feelings of guilt and anxiety have been eliminated. To this extent we have opened our self system to a new input from the reality which surrounds us.[1]

While the various training methods under discussion share a common base with some forms of psychotherapy, there are important differences among them. These lie mainly in (1) the nature of the subject matter employed, (2) the degree of personal involvement, and (3) the outcomes of training.

SUBJECT MATTER USED

The subject matter of the case method of human relations training always includes clinical material taken from life situations. It is based on a record of activities, interactions, and emotions or feelings involving people other than those present in the training session. This behavior has a locus "out there" or "there and then," as contrasted with the activities, interactions, and emotions which are generated "here and now" among those participating in laboratory training. In the latter type of training, the subject matter emerges spontaneously, as we pointed out. With nothing to divert them and encouraged by the trainer to do so, the participants discuss themselves, their relationships to each other and the situation, and the personal and organizational obstacles which seem to them to be impeding easier and more meaningful interpersonal, intragroup, and intergroup relations.

However, it should not be concluded that the case method focuses exclusively on "out there" behavior and that laboratory training concerns itself only with "here and now" behavior. From the standpoint of subject matter it would be more

---

[1] It is clear that this learning sequence may be discussed from either an external or an internal frame of reference. One can emphasize that data from the environment have brought one's attitudes into question (upsetting experience). In the individual's effort to feel more in tune with the environment, these attitudes have been altered—leading to behavioral changes. Or one can emphasize that perceptual changes (choices) have occurred, leading to a new concept of self in relation to others which in turn, has brought about changes in behavior. We have chosen the latter point of view.

accurate to visualize these two methods as lying along a continuum with each method in its pure form located at the opposite ends, in Fig. 4. Toward the center of the continuum the two methods merge and cross over into the primary territory of the other. In other words, laboratory training sometimes gets involved in the problems of organizational change in which some "there and then" data are used, while the case method sometimes gets involved in consideration of personal attitudes and feelings in which some "here and now" data must be used. In fact, in some of its forms, laboratory training structures its sessions around hypothetical situations, film dramas, role-playing, or even philosophical issues. Any one of these may provide the vehicle for exploring personal ideas, beliefs, attitudes, and values, and suggesting new direction for them. By the same token, the case method often uses role-playing in accordance with the case situation but designed to demonstrate and analyze the personal behavior of the participants. In the main, however, the primary focus of laboratory training is on the participants themselves, while that of the case method is with analysis of prepared clinical materials.

Role-playing, as a training device, would be located on the imaginary subject-matter continuum somewhere between the points occupied by the case method and laboratory training. A typical role-playing situation might be as follows:

You are the boss. Your secretary has been late several times since you hired her about six months ago. You are irritated when you arrive before she does. On the other hand, she has been very efficient and likeable in other ways, and you want to keep her if you can.

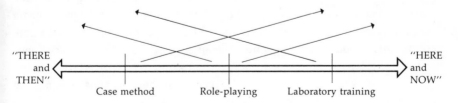

Fig. 4. Subject matter continuum.

She was late again this morning, and you are wondering what you ought to do about it. You decide to have a talk with her. What would you say?

It can be seen that this situation contains in it elements of "there and then" behavior—yours and your secretary's past attitudes and behavior in the office. When the scene is played out with one person taking the role of the boss and another that of the secretary, "here and now" behavior will be generated. The resultant interaction will be a synthesis of both kinds of behavior. Each person will play a part which combines his or her own predispositions toward the dilemmas presented, but at the same time will be constrained by the situation as given.

Role-playing, depending upon its design, may also move in one direction or another along the continuum shown in Fig. 4. A role-play situation which is aimed at learning a skill such as chairing a meeting using Roberts's *Rules of Order* would lie nearer to the left end of the continuum. On the other hand, role-playing as a form of therapy, as it is sometimes used in the treatment of mental disturbances, would lie near the right end.

LEVEL OF INVOLVEMENT

In the case method, the level of involvement, that is, the extent to which exposure of the personal self or "I" takes place, is controllable both by the individual participant and by the teacher or trainer. The presence of a subject matter which is objective (case) and the range of behavior available to the trainer make a lower level of psychological "risk" possible. The primary attention of the participants is on the case rather than on each other. This tends to reduce explicit interpersonal interaction and to shield inner feelings. Also, the individual participant can to some extent enter into or withdraw from sensitive self-issues by projecting his own feelings and attitudes upon the people in the case, thus escaping the embarassment of revealing in "me" those aspects of "I" which he may desire to hide.

Opportunities to explore and possibly to relieve personal inner feelings of conflict and frustration are not ordinarily present in this type of training unless it is supplemented by individual and/or group conferences especially arranged for this purpose. A great deal depends upon the particular outcomes the trainer has in mind. He may vary the level of involvement (voluntarily or involuntarily) by the extent to which he succeeds in creating a "safe" atmosphere among the participants in the training sessions. If both the participants and the trainer, however, are willing and, in the case of the latter, capable, consideration of "here and now" issues can be as intensive in the case method as may be desired. The subject matter can be shifted from the case material to the behavior of the participants and, perhaps, of the trainer.

Involvement in laboratory training means explicit self-exposure. "I" and "me," as perceived both by the individual and his "others," are brought out into the open. The purpose of this type of training is re-education by promoting opportunities for the participants to explore "I" in a supportive atmosphere and to observe and evaluate "me" in action through the reflected reactions of others. Thus the parallel here to psychotherapy is very close, although as we said earlier, the purpose and clientele are different. Behavior changes are sought through altering the ways in which the participants respond to their environment, particularly to the "here and now" environment that comprises the patterns of interpersonal relationships which develop in the laboratory. It is necessary that participants confront themselves and each other at deep personal levels where intrinsic attitudes and values form the core of personality. Figure 5 provides a diagram picturing the relative degree of personal involvement of various training methods.

Thus we can see that in role-playing, which contains elements of both "here and now" and "there and then" behavior, the level of involvement is relatively "safer" than in the T-group mode of laboratory training. Although an objective of role-playing is to provide participants with an opportunity to "be themselves" within the constraints of the structured aspects of their role, there is, nevertheless, an equal opportunity to escape into the role itself. "That is not me, that is only a role I am playing" is a way of reducing the anxieties and

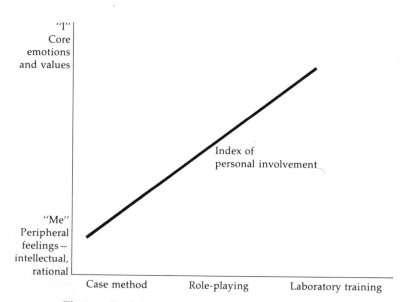

Fig. 5.   Training methods and levels of involvement.

of pacifying defensive reactions whenever sensitive areas of the self seem threatened. In fact, for this very reason, role-players often feel less inhibited when experimenting with different behaviors than they might in the "real world" of the T-group experience.

THE OUTCOMES OF TRAINING

The object of the training procedures we have been discussing (case method, role-playing, and laboratory training) is to change behavior by improving analytical and social skills and, in some instances, by increasing self-awareness and changing attitudes toward self and others. Changing behavior by increasing a person's knowledge about certain ideas and objects is a common educational procedure. As one learns new facts, new behavior becomes possible unless the new facts are in some way "changed" or altered by a set of related attitudes or beliefs already present in the self structure. Most people (though not all!) can learn the emotionally neutral skills required to drive an automobile, or can acquire the knowledge needed to use the multiplication tables. However, in most situations attitudes derived from such sources as parents, reference groups, or one's status in society act as filters, alter perceptions, and influence behavior accordingly.

Attitudes are sometimes defined as predispositions to act in certain ways in the presence of specific ideas or objects. Sometimes they are defined as views or convictions. Sometimes they are shown in terms of preferences for certain beliefs or courses of action, e.g., being permissive rather than controlling with respect to children or students, or preferring a liberal over a conservative approach to politics. However, our behavior in any given instance results from a complex mix of positive and negative attitudes derived from our history and from short-term influences of time or place. Thus the relationship of attitudes to behavior is rarely a simple one.

This relationship has been demonstrated in a variety of ways by psychologists. Behavior, being visible to others, is more flexible than attitudes. Cultural norms often require us to be polite whether we wish to be or not, to defer to older people whether we respect them or not, and on many occasions to keep adverse opinions to ourselves when we are bursting with the desire to speak our minds. We are also aware of the numerous occasions when we know what is right but do what is wrong, e.g., we argue with others to obey the speed limit while frequently violating it ourselves. To complicate things even further, attitudes do not always precede behavior. Sometimes they change *as a result* of behavior, as in the case of a person whose habit of smoking makes him refuse to concede that cancer and smoking are related. Attitude change can also be a consequence of a role-playing experience similar to those described earlier.

These complex relationships between our attitudes and our behavior also affect the very training processes we are discussing. For example, culturally held attitudes of disapproval about exposing one's feelings can be detrimental to learning. We cannot know how useful or how accurate such feelings may be unless we expose them and exchange information about them. The effect on attitudes of playing a role under controlled conditions has already been discussed.

Attitudes are more susceptible to change when we are deeply interested and find ourselves caught in an ambiguous situation. In other words, when, in a T-group, or in role-playing where group norms require us to expose our inner selves and where we find through feedback that our attitudes are inconsistent or inexplicable in relation to our self-concept, we experience feelings of anxiety. If the environment is supportive and our concern is high, we can perhaps avoid defensive reactions as we try to overcome the inconsistency or the feeling of ambiguity which troubles us.

The outcomes or personal changes to be expected from the various methods of training will vary with the level of involvement. Where the "there and then" remains the focus of discussion, cognitive changes or an increase in knowledge may be expected to occur in social behavior as participants adapt to the social situation in the discussions group. Cognitive changes will also take place in the participants' knowledge about social and psychological phenomena. Members of the group will become more aware of personal values and their influence on interpersonal effectiveness. In addition, they will develop such basic skills as observing, diagnosing "out there" behaviors, and taking effective action. Unless, however, the participants seek and the trainer introduces into the discussion or in private conferences intensive consideration of "here and now" behavior, changes in values and therefore in personal core behavior will not take place. In other words, cognitive changes may occur which affect "me" but effect little or no change in "I."

Maintaining a lower level of personal involvement, a usual characteristic of the case method and role-playing approaches (the latter to a lesser degree) is both an advantage and a disadvantage when compared with more inclusive forms of personal training. The training situation may be deliberately designed to deal with core values and attitudes that constitute serious barriers to needed personal growth and development. The outcome should be more effective behavior.

The specific purpose of laboratory training is to alter personal values, improve interpersonal skills, and increase the effectiveness of groups in achieving their goals. Sometimes work focuses on only one of these purposes, sometimes on all simultaneously. Thus, the outcomes of laboratory training are related to positive changes in levels of awareness, in communications skills, openness to experience, emotional adjustment, sensitivity, and other aspects of normal personality development and improved interpersonal relations. Laboratory training tends to achieve these results at deeper personal levels as the participants in fact have agreed to become involved on a personal level rather than in terms of a situation "out there."

THE CONCEPTUAL FRAMEWORK OF THE CHANGE PROCESS

Change, then, is a process which requires (1) building upon the individual's capacity to change himself and (2) a special kind of relationship between the change agent or agents and the changee or changees. People have the capacity to learn new ways of thinking and acting and to respond in kind to a supportive interpersonal climate. Although an individual may have developed a more or less fixed personality, he need not always remain "hung up" at some point on the dependency-independency scale, for example, and always respond to and use "authority" in ways which he learned as a child. As we stated in Chapter 3, man must find his path as he relates to things and people. Ideally, he should succeed in reaching a level where he is able to feel and act in accordance with his potential for contributing to constructive human life. Men will cooperate when they find helping behavior in other men. In our view, to say that human nature is essentially fixed and unchangeable, as some social scientists do, is to say that man has no potential for development and growth.

In Fig. 6 we have diagrammed the general conceptual framework of the various change methods which meet our criteria, showing their relationship to other social processes concerned with change. All start from an existential-humanistic base, or what is essentially a pilot view of human nature (1). The basic assumption is that man's tendency toward good can be made to prevail and that, *given the opportunity*, he can make sound decisions concerning himself and in cooperation with others engage in constructive and supportive behavior.

In (2) "client-centered therapy", we show the fundamental Rogerian process of psychotherapy. The responsibility for exploring and resolving his problems, i.e., changing his attitudes and learning new behaviors, is placed in the client. Ideally, he responds to a complex set of needs which result in an effort to self-actualize or to move toward his total potential as a person. The therapist in this system of psychotherapy assumes a "helping relationship" in which he supports the client by empathizing with him. The client, through a process of relating to the therapist, reviews and replaces the less useful aspects of his initial value system (largely borrowed from others in earlier experience) and discovers constructive new ways of relating to others.

Rogerian psychotherapy is included in Fig. 6 because of its seminal relationship to the training procedures discussed in this chapter. This technique is characterized by self-impelled learning approaches and shares many of the values we have outlined in these pages, such as acceptance, participation opportunity, freedom of communication, a supportive psychological climate, and experimentation. Our emphasis, of course, has been on the application of these conditions to everyday interpersonal relations in organizational life.

The case method of human relations training, role-playing, and laboratory training are shown in (3), (4), and (5) and have already been discussed. Also shown are two processes which are a part of the same philosophical and procedural family. These are the administrative processes of group decision-making and participative management (6). Both of these also depend on the premise that individuals and groups have the capacity to make sound choices within their range of knowledge and that a supportive, facilitative leadership climate can bring this capacity out.

Group decision-making and participative management are often used synonymously to mean the practice of organizational democracy. Both are concerned with the decentralization of decision-making power in organizations. This, of course, means the personal involvement of individuals at all appropriate levels in the determination of group organizational goals and the means by which they are to be reached.

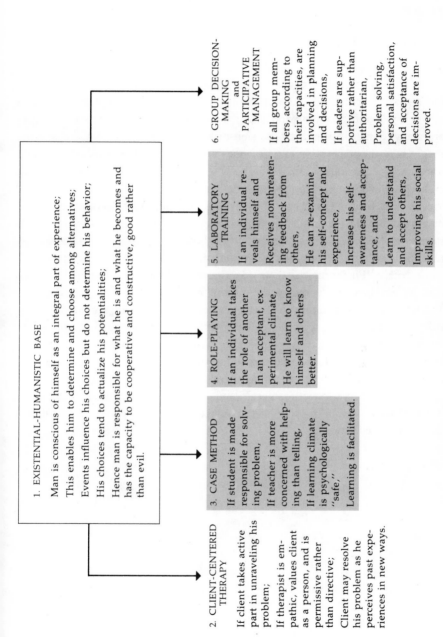

1. EXISTENTIAL-HUMANISTIC BASE

Man is conscious of himself as an integral part of experience;

This enables him to determine and choose among alternatives;

Events influence his choices but do not determine his behavior;

His choices tend to actualize his potentialities;

Hence man is responsible for what he is and what he becomes and has the capacity to be cooperative and constructive, good rather than evil.

2. CLIENT-CENTERED THERAPY

If client takes active part in unraveling his problem;

If therapist is empathic, values client as a person, and is permissive rather than directive;

Client may resolve his problem as he perceives past experiences in new ways.

3. CASE METHOD

If student is made responsible for solving problem,

If teacher is more concerned with helping than telling,

If learning climate is psychologically "safe,"

Learning is facilitated.

4. ROLE-PLAYING

If an individual takes the role of another

In an acceptant, experimental climate,

He will learn to know himself and others better.

5. LABORATORY TRAINING

If an individual reveals himself and

Receives nonthreatening feedback from others,

He can re-examine his self-concept and experience,

Increase his self-awareness and acceptance, and

Learn to understand and accept others,

Improving his social skills.

6. GROUP DECISION-MAKING and PARTICIPATIVE MANAGEMENT

If all group members, according to their capacities, are involved in planning and decisions,

If leaders are supportive rather than authoritarian,

Problem solving, personal satisfaction, and acceptance of decisions are improved.

Fig. 6. Conceptual framework of various change processes.

Although some theoreticians believe that the application of group decision-making and participation creates more problems than it solves, the arguments for a clearer understanding and use of these forms of organizational democracy are many. It means delegating decision-making to where the *knowledge* is rather than where the *power* is. In our tradition-bound organizational society, this idea sometimes causes raised eye-brows because it implies that people lower in the organization can know more about some things than those higher up. Nevertheless, as this book has constantly reiterated, the quality of decisions can often be improved if the total human potential for creativity is utilized. Group decision-making also affords people an opportunity to become ego-involved, i.e., personally identified with their tasks, and consequently motivates them to perform their work better. Furthermore, their identification with the group in decisions concerning their work, makes them more inclined to support such decisions and to accept responsibility for them. An added plus is that people who are involved in the ongoing processes of production are prepared to accept change more readily, simply because they are in the mainstream and can anticipate essential change. Finally, the necessary supportive or facilitative roles which leaders must play in group decisions—and these are the roles which this book is all about—help to create better morale and better working relationships among organizational members. The result is greater individual and organizational growth and development.

CHAPTER NINE

THE BUREAUCRATIC ENVIRONMENT OF LEADERSHIP

"Leadership is the fulcrum on which the demands of the individual and the demands of the organization are balanced."

WARREN BENNIS

Up to this point we have discussed leadership as a product of interaction between individuals, and we have placed primary emphasis on its psychological dimensions. The leader has been viewed as one who functions as a catalyst for cooperation and communication and as one who performs the role of change agent in relation to the members of the organization. There are, however, sociological dimensions to leadership, dimensions which, in effect, provide the context within which the leader carries out his functions. These dimensions include, first the formal structure or blueprint of organization, second, the informal or emergent organization which caters to the human needs of membership and stresses the notion of diffused or situational leadership, and, finally, the distribution of power and authority.

THE ORGANIZATIONAL ENVIRONMENT OF THE LEADER

In an organization which exists as an instrument for achieving designated objectives, we look for the leadership which generates course and direction. We will use the term *formal organization* to refer to an instrumentality for action only. It is composed of a hierarchical authority structure where authority is conferred on the incumbent by virtue of his position. This organization is task-oriented as reflected in the pre-planned horizontal and vertical divisions of work. Members of top management, including the chief executive or the founder-owner of the enterprise, perform a critical role in the formulation of objectives and goals of the formal organization. They are assumed to possess the knowledge and wisdom to design its structure and to provide the mechanisms for its successful performance.

For the entrepreneurial organization, ownership and management coincide. Therefore, whatever the owner regards as furthering his personal goals will, in fact, be translated into the goals of the business. If we assume personal profit maximization as an important goal of the owner-founder, this becomes also an important objective of the firm he heads.

In the large complex organization, which is publicly owned, management is separated from the ownership of the enterprise. Maximization of personal long-run financial or nonfinancial rewards for the professional managers may or may not serve the best interests of the organization which they head. This type of management is characterized by a high level of influence and authority, but this influence and authority must be relinquished when the executive leaves his position and no longer commands the resources of the organization. The identical condition applies to the members of management of a hospital, a government agency, a church, the military, and to other organizations which employ professional managers.

An *informal* organization exists as an integral part of the formal organization. The moment the organization as an instrumentality is off the drawing board and the first members have joined it, the informal organization begins to emerge spontaneously as a reflection of the human condition. Just as man in an ancient past joined with other tribal members to assure his protection, survival, maintenance, and procreation, he now replicates this experience of the natural environment within the organizational environment. He joins hands with fellow employees in an informal community or group created to serve age-old human needs for protection, security, and companionship, in short, for a way of life that promises a means of meeting human needs which is not available within the formal structure's prescribed relationships. It is important for managers and subordinates alike to recognize that, as human beings (the focus of this book) they are members of such informal organizations—irrational, in contrast to the rationality of the formal structure, and governed by the feelings, sentiments, emotions, and divergent values of their members.

Thus those in authority can decide, command, or act, as is appropriate to chiefs or heads in organizational hierarchies, but their authority becomes effective only in the hands of managers displaying appropriate personal abilities and capacities, i.e., influence and power. Authority is attached to position; influence and power are attached to person. By influence we refer mainly to a person's ability to control the rewards of others, while power reflects a person's ability to suspend another person's discretionary decision-making behavior, judgment, or evaluation through control of rewards and punishments.

While it is quite possible for a person to claim for himself a position of authority, including whatever title it bestows on him, he cannot lay claim either to power or leadership except as he demonstrates them and causes others to accept them as such. Thus, as we indicated previously, both power and leadership rest with a person and with the informal organization.

The formal organization is an ordered authority structure which implicitly establishes legitimate channels of communication and lines of advancement and promotion. In contrast, the informal organization includes a much greater variety of organizational forms as overlays upon the formal organization. Thus, the informal organization comprises multiple structural relationships. Each one of us has relied, for example, on the structure of the informal communication network or "grapevine" for information perhaps not available within the official information network of the organization. Likewise, we have used and have felt the influence of the organization's power structure, decision-making structure of functional expertise, and friendship structure. All these structures exist within the informal organization and serve the needs of its members.

Since we have a number of such structures in the informal organization, more than one leader or one focal point for leadership must exist. As we grow up with the prevailing perceptions and viewpoints of our environment, we may easily grant a leadership role to a person because of physical traits, which in our culture are interpreted as granting a person superiority. Thus, height alone may convey a visual image of leadership, as may authoritative manners of speech and behavior, superior intelligence, and so on. Such trait characteristics may be decisive in bestowing leadership upon a person in a situation where performance cannot easily be measured, in friendship situations, for example, and in other socially defined situations. In contrast, the demands of a particular situation may call forth a hitherto unknown leader because of his ability to provide the personal and organizational qualities the situation demands, e.g., facilitating the satisfaction of changing group needs according to the situation. The old scoutmaster replaces the social scion after the luxury yacht is shipwrecked on a desolate island!

Following our contention that a leader emerges only to the extent that he has followers who accept his leadership, none of the traits discussed may be relevant to his role nor may the situation be defined in terms of performance criteria. Instead, the leader may emerge as a result of being part of a group process which generates organizational needs for its membership and validates the position of leadership for a particular member of the group. Such leader-generating group processes include the various forms of representative elections in democratically run organizations. The group process also explains why holders of positions of authority in the organization find support for their leadership even though other men in the organization appear to have more potential leadership to offer in terms of personal traits or the demands of the situation.

As an illustration of formal and informal organization familiar to all of us, we may consider the family in Western society.

Traditionally, we have tended to think of the organization of the family as consisting of the father as head of the household, his wife as next in command, and, in her role as mother, having immediate supervision of the children. We also recognize the sometime variant of this where grandparents, under the concept of the extended family, in fact are an integral part of the total family organization with the position of family head residing in the grandfather on the father's side. In these simplistic terms the organization chart for the family may be pictured as follows:

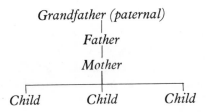

However, it is quite clear that this formal organization of the family is relevant only in certain highly restrictive terms concerned with matters of law. Even legal definitions are not uniformly applied from state to state or from nation to nation. Also, we have experienced significant changes in familial roles. The grandparental generation has disappeared almost totally from the typical family organization in the urban, industrialized areas of the United States. The husband, more and more, is being relegated to the breadwinner role, while the wife is assuming a position of authority and decision-making in the allocation of the family's income among competing needs and temptations. And developments—not to mention the Women's Liberation Front—suggest even further strengthening of the wife's role as a coequal with the husband. In the background may still lurk the influential image of mother-in-law, more often the wife's mother since sons are likely to leave home and sever family ties more completely than daughters do. Finally, many contend that the recent period of permissiveness in child rearing has made the United States child-oriented to such a degree that the children in the family, particularly the teenagers, assert themselves and dictate to their parents. If they are not in the driver's seat, they at least have equal access to it.

The informal organization of the family has always reflected the individual capacity and capability of its various members, the demands of various situations, and the mutual arrangements and agreements for the proper functioning and survival of the family unit and the support of its individual members. Thus, the intelligent wife and mother has probably always exercised leadership far beyond the rights provided her by law. Similarly, sons and daughters who have been endowed with superior intellects or provided with the opportunity for advanced education, assume leadership in particular instances. They may, for example, take the responsibility for income tax preparation or investment decisions for the family. The leadership of parents may also be abrogated if some other person, a friend or relative, overshadows the parents in their influence on family members. Finally, the institution of the family in society, of course, reflects a base of values which make up a nation's culture and belief system. These values are injected into the workings of the family apart from unilateral decision-making by any single member or by the family as a whole. Society ascribes to the family the role of providing support and a prescribed minimum education for its children. In addition to discharging the responsibilities of providing a home, the family is expected to teach values related to ethical and moral behavior.

Thus, organizations wherever they are found, in business, in the family, in government, etc., show many parallels in so far as formal and informal structural relationships are concerned. They also show differences due to their diverse objectives and values. These differences should be recognized and accounted for, and indeed at times deliberately sustained against the onslaught of behavior patterns of seemingly similar and more successful organizations. In the remote past the business organization of the craftsman's shop clearly reflected the structure of the family. The family of today, tied more closely to industry and commerce, is itself heavily influenced in many of its judgments and decisions by the values of the modern business organization. The appropriateness of this condition has only recently begun to attract our attention in evaluating the role of the family in modern society.

THE WEBERIAN LEADERSHIP TYPOLOGY

It may be helpful to review at this point Max Weber's conclusion that the source of leadership can be traced to three separate forms of organizational situations, each conferring authority on the leader in relation to other organizational members. Tradition governs how the society or organization is ruled in situations where it has existed for a long time. The hereditary chieftain or king reflects tradition as a source of leadership legitimacy by the prevailing definitions of leadership in that culture.

Thus, Malaysia is ruled by a prime minister, but the titular head of the state is a king who is elected for four years. However, this election takes place only among hereditary rulers of regional subdivisions who thus pass the honor of being king around themselves and thereby preserve for the king something beyond the reach of the ordinary commoner.

However, the superiority of an individual may become apparent as a result of his charisma "by grace of God," his magnetism as a person, or his zealous fervor for a cause. These may all call forth followers who accept him as their leader because they believe in him. Such charismatic leadership is frequently found in revolutionary leaders. Note also the possible parallel in the dimensions of the charismatic leadership form with the leaders of the informal organization generally.

Weber suggested that where a charismatic leader has achieved a position of power, he must establish a legal-rational structure in order to deliver on the promises he has made to his followers and to retain his position. (In the informal structures we have discussed previously, there was, of course, no such emphasis on formalism.) This legal-rational structure or bureaucracy becomes the seat of authority which is attached to position by virtue of a charter of existence. Legitimization may have been granted to the organization by its founder or by the state. This chartered bureaucracy is then committed to the impersonal distribution of goods and services according to a rational plan. We recognize in this legal-rational structure the dimensions of the formal organization.

This formal organization or legal-rational or bureaucratic structure is the source of legitimation of force and thus of power. We recognize, therefore, that holders of power, in their efforts to legitimize it, seek to become incumbents of positions conferring upon them equivalent authority. We also recognize with Weber a circular process as we contemplate the likelihood that the following flow will take place.

The *legal-rational* bureaucratic structure will revert to a

traditional base for organizational operations, and that this, with
the appearance of

leadership dynamic for change will be followed by the inevitable

entrepreneurial, innovative, revolutionary phase, and that this, in
turn, will be followed by the

routinization of charisma or charismatic leadership, and eventually
by a

legal-rational bureaucracy.

Leadership functions in a rational world of bureaucratic forms, prescribed procedures, and hierarchical authority. It also functions in an irrational setting of emergent human interactions, activities, and sentiments—irrational, that is, in relation to the grand design or plan of the organization. For Weber, we must hasten to add, bureaucracy or the legal-rational structure was a tool for analyzing and interpreting social phenomena. It literally was organization for the classification and manipulation of data by means of which social structures could be compared with the "ideal." It was not intended to be used as a model for action.

The main arena of action for the leader is the informal or emergent organization which is composed of human values and patterns of behavior not covered by rules and arising naturally from the interactions of persons as they go about their daily tasks. These are the everyday, day-in and day-out, face-to-face encounters through which flesh and blood members attempt to translate into goal-seeking action the rational order of the formal organization. This goal-seeking activity gives life to the skeletal social structure and the prescribed relationships. It is here that leadership, whatever its variety and style, is practiced. For it is here that the leader, through his influence and power rather than through any ordained position of authority, must use his capacity to mold and change the course of human activity.

CHAPTER TEN

THE CHALLENGE OF SYNERGISTIC LEADERSHIP

"I shall call this . . . synergy, the old term used . . . to mean combined action . . . greater than the run of their separate actions."

RUTH BENEDICT

At the beginning of this work we expressed our belief that the key to better organizational effectiveness would be found in new forms of interpersonal relations among members of the organization. These new types of interpersonal relations are particularly critical in the leader-follower relationship, upon which depends the success or failure of a task-oriented society. They are characterized by attitudes of cooperation based upon feelings of mutual trust and openness which provide the basis for synergy among individuals in the organization. Such organizational orientation is in marked contrast to traditional patterns of competitiveness and impersonality, which are frequently destructive and negative in their dimensions. This *derogatory syndrome*, or this condition of low synergy, to use Ruth Benedict's term, is symptomatic of much of competitive and professional life today, rather than the high synergy we visualize as an imperative of modern man in organizations both now and for the future.

Competition between business firms or between vendors and buyers of goods and services has been a vitalizing factor in the material success of the Western industrialized nations, particularly of the United States. However, when the competitive spirit invades those areas of human relations where competition is inappropriate and cooperation is called for—and such invasions appear inevitable as a consequence of the urge to get ahead—men, as mere instruments of the institutions they represent, are wasted or devoured before their time.

James Reston, a perceptive social and political commentator, recently re-marked in the *New York Times* on the difficulties faced by the President of the United States in filling key government jobs with men from private walks of life. He said:

Everywhere today one hears the complaint, even in the universities, that the struggle to get ahead and even to manage one small part of a great (organizational) machine, leaves a man little time to think about what he is doing or even to reflect on the purpose of the enterprise or institution he serves."

We are convinced that men who are in positions of leadership are worn down more by the quality of the human relationships they must endure and which they do not know how to handle than they are by the technical problems of their assign-ments. This is evident from the symptoms of tension and frustration to be found everywhere in our organizational society—manifestations of hypertension, alcoholism, divorce, premature resignations from the rat race in the executive suites, and the refusal of many individuals to meet the demands of organizations or the needs of society in general. The challenge of leadership in management calls for a review of the dimensions of the derogatory syndrome, and a realization of the need for a new emphasis on synergistic human relationships.

LEADERSHIP AS A SOURCE OF VALUES

Leadership represents an elite which acts as a value carrier to be emulated by the other members of the organization, and functions to conserve whatever values prevail. From our previous discussion, we can see that the informal organization and its various components form an expression of values of the members of the organization. The formal organization and its management can formulate the objectives and goals and the organizational plan of the enterprise, but only leader-ship can provide values for the organization which will enable it to become an institution, an end worthy in itself. The survival of the informal organization is an end in itself as is any organization which exists as a community and as an instrumentality of survival of each of its members.

At this point the analytical distinction between formal and informal organization disappears because management also acts as an elite for the formal organization and thus injects into its *raison d'être* the prevailing values of the management group, of the chief executive, or of the founder-owner of the organization, as the case may be. Philip Selznick suggested that only to the extent that management is successful in translating the objectives and goals of the organization to values, do men acquire the qualities of statesmanship when they become heads and leaders of institutions. At such a point, the analytical differentiation between formal and informal organization can no longer be maintained because these now fuse and involve a total personal commitment to the organization's values on the part of the membership. Thus, the organization becomes an end in itself while at the same time remaining an instrument of its membership. This outcome is in contrast to the condition in our earlier discussion where the informal organization could, at times, involve itself in security operations on behalf of its members, operations that could be detrimental to the realization of the objectives and goals of the formal organization. By definition, if the organization becomes value-laden for its members, the organization and all it stands for has become worth while. It assumes, then, a position in member's ideal and operational value hierarchy.

So far we have discussed the leader and leadership as they emerge in an environment of individual and organizational behavior. The leader in effect performs the function of crystallizing the values of his organization and also of interpreting, conserving, and changing these values. When we refer to dynamic leadership we refer to a leader who is functioning as an agent of change. It follows that he is of critical importance in creating an image which characterizes the organization and to which individuals as members are expected to conform. As a result, the members, given a long enough exposure to an organizational environment or through a process of self-selection, will internalize the values held by their superiors to the extent that the latter exercise effective leadership. The style of leadership which characterizes managers and, in particular, the chief executive, will in turn characterize the organizational climate as a whole.

STYLE OF LEADERSHIP

The kind of leader an individual is reflects his personality and the processes of development and growth which have affected it. The style of leadership thus must be regarded in terms of the underlying personality characteristics of the manager. Just as the manager's impressions and recollections of authority figures in his past became an integral part of his personality, he in turn, critically influences his subordinates and the growth and development of their personalities.

Much of the original work related to leadership style was done in 1939 by Kurt Lewin, Ronald Lippitt, and Ralph White in connection with studies at the Institute of Child Development at the University of Iowa. The relevant experiment, although completed more than thirty years ago, is worth being retold for its brevity and clarity in illustrating our discussion.

Lewin and his associates conceived the idea of using a group of boys in the 9–12 age group to demonstrate the impact of different styles of leadership on social organizations. They designated adult leaders for three separate groups and specified the leadership style or leadership behavior each leader was to exhibit in his dealings with the boys under his control. In each case the group was engaged in a carpentry task involving the making of parts from blueprints supplied by the leader. Then the experimenters rigged up a room in which they hid a film camera to record events in the group.

For the first group, the three scientists provided a climate characterized by a laissez-faire style of leadership. The adult leader is seen entering the room, drawings in his hands, with instructions to be totally passive and noncommital in interacting with the group. He takes a seat against the wall of the room and throws up his hands as to what steps the boys should take in proceeding toward task completion. Clearly, all the information is on the drawing, all they need to do is pick it up. After a while, the adult leader leaves the room. The moment he disappears, the boys slip out one by one. When the leader returns, he returns to an empty room, the task incomplete.

In the second group we see the adult leader enter and immediately proceed to hand out jobs to be performed by each boy. The leader is authoritative in his manner, and whenever anyone runs out of work, the leader has a new assignment for him. The place hums, the boys are working, and the leader is in complete control of the situation. Then he leaves the room for a moment. Immediately all work stops, fisticuffs ensue, and a great free-for-all seems to provide an outlet for pent-up emotions which had been lurking waiting for release. The leader re-enters, quickly restores order and peace, and the work proceeds, the task is completed. The experimenters referred to this style of leadership as autocratic.

Finally, for the third group, the leader brings with him the drawing of the item to be made by the boys, and proceeds in an easy-going friendly manner to invite commitments to specific aspects of the total assignment, and to suggest tasks to be performed by those not sure of what they want to do. He takes a seat against the wall of the room but is helpful with suggestions when he is asked for comments, and when work seems to slack off, he encourages the group to go on. When the leader leaves the room, nothing unusual happens, work continues as before, the leader re-enters, and the work is completed. For this style of leadership, the Lewin group chose the term democratic.

The laissez-faire style of leadership is not relevant to an organizational environment which is goal-oriented and task-oriented. Rather it suggests abdication of management and leadership—as may frequently happen at managerial levels where staff specialists appear and preempt all aspects of planning, give expert advice, and make decisions to the point where little opportunity is left for the manager himself to exercise active authority. Management may also contribute to this state of affairs by becoming highly centralized at the top with minimum delegation of authority and responsibility downward in the organization.

It is also all too easy to fall into the same trap with some writers in our democratic culture, who have a social or behavioral science background and who often carry through a discussion of leadership with the implicit suggestion that a manager worth his salt must overnight acquire a democratic style of leadership. These writers frequently relate this style of leadership to criteria of efficiency and productivity. The alert reader soon discovers, however, that correlation of these criteria with style of leadership may be uncertain or nonexistent, suggesting that the discussion really ought to have been carried out in ideological terms which would reflect the writer's bias.

Leadership style is a product of individual development over time and cannot be easily changed. In moments of stress, in particular, the false colors of the counterfeit always show through, and the power and image of leadership diminishes, accordingly. Thus, in an earlier chapter, we discussed several available training methods, based upon principles of re-education, which seem to us to hold out hope that, *given the proper conditions and time*, leadership style may be altered. This judgment is based upon an optimistic view of human nature—the view that man has within himself the power to reconsider, to choose, to adjust, to adapt, and, therefore, to move in directions of personal growth which will enhance his potentialities. This conviction is something more than an ideology, since it has, at least in part, some empirical basis derived from personal experience and observation, the reports of students, the opinions of experienced practitioners involved in organizational change programs, as well as admittedly scanty but generally positive research evidence.

In today's changing world there is a need for managers to pursue the elusive goal of change, personal change, wherever their natural leadership styles defeat or discourage the principle of synergy or *working together*. Managers need, at the least, to know where their personalities fit on the range of leadership styles and to recognize that certain consequences can be anticipated. If they would escape the label of manipulator, however, this is only the beginning. Self-awareness and personal change go deeper than mere intellectual curiosity and mental calculation. They reach into the shadows of the mind seeking discovery and control of hitherto unknown aspects of the personality. The successful leader needs to find and accept himself in order to be sensitive and responsive to the full range of needs in his environment. In no other way can he adapt himself effectively to the demands of a changing organizational society.

THE IMPACT OF LEADERSHIP ON THE INDIVIDUAL

Now that we have explored the implications of leadership for the organization as a whole and reflected upon the leader as a person, we will turn our attention to the effect of the leader and leadership style on the individual member of the organization. Our major proposition is that leadership significantly determines the personal development and growth of the led and frequently is the prime factor in an individual's decision to remain with the organization rather than to leave it.

In being concerned with the leader from the point of view of a member of the organization, we are focusing on a dimension similar to the dimensions of social culture and social structure. We noted earlier the contention of the biologist Allee that in every group a hierarchy or pecking order tends to become established. In any organizational environment there is a continuing process of evaluation of an individual's capacity and ability in terms of task performance and social interaction. As the pecking order emerges, the leader represents an accepted and acceptable path-finder and pacesetter to the individual organization member. He becomes implicitly if not explicitly one more link in the chain of authority figures to which any person is subject throughout his life. Some authority figures exercise their capacity to narrow the individual's choices by virtue of their position, others do so by virtue of superior intellect, fitness in terms of situational requirements, self-awareness, and sensitivity, or as a result of the group processes we discussed earlier.

However, in addition to characteristics which are more or less open to investigation, the successful leader represents something more to his followers. He represents a quality that primitive man explained as magic, but that we, in our age of science, think of as consistency of values and ethical concern. The leader reflects a charisma which instills an implicit belief in his followers that he can and will succeed, and that their interest lies in his interest. The leader provides the symbol for the collectivity represented by the organization, and thus an internalization of the norms according to which the organization functions. The leader therefore sets the course for the organization to follow and becomes in his behavior the standard or ideal which will be emulated and imitated in the organization by its members. Thus the leader's values become the values of the organization and its membership.

SYNERGY THROUGH LEADERSHIP

The leader through his personality may reflect an autocratic or a democratic style of leadership. His posture will determine whether the organization's members have an opportunity for development and growth in their own personalities. If we recall that father figures and other authority figures represent one of the most important determinants of personality, the importance to an individual of his relationship to a leader is evident. The leader should reflect in his leadership style a willingness to have trust and confidence in those around him, thus creating for them a basis on which to build their individual confidence and security. A managerial philosophy of decentralization, if fully developed, allows the individual members of the organization to have access to as much authority and responsibility as they choose to undertake. In turn they are encouraged to demonstrate in their own behavior with their co-workers and subordinates trust and confidence in carrying out the organization's objectives and goals. Under these circumstances, each individual can identify his success with his personal capacity and abilities. He is encouraged to look ahead to even greater responsibilities insofar as he is willing to identify himself with the objectives and goals of the organization. In this way the synergy of the individual members and the organization itself is formed. It is in accord with the needs of modern man in a changing organizational society.

In a situation where information flows freely and relationships reflect power equalization, we are dealing with an open organization. This provides a climate that fosters the development of professionalism on the part of members. It encourages the growth of attributes and the attitudes associated with a life path where each individual's goals are compatible with the performance of his work. The leader is only one among the many, although perhaps *primus inter pares*; he relies on persuasion and open communication to achieve self-discipline and self-control on the part of the others in the drive toward the organization's objectives and goals.

For the individual, the environment created by a leader who encourages individual development and growth is not without frustrations. As in any democratic organization, aspirations and hopes are aroused which may be beyond reach of the person in terms of his abilities. If hopes are aroused but the goals are not realized, the members of the organization may react in one of two ways. They may feel rejected by the organization and regress to attitudes of apathy and defeatism or they may react with aggression, hostility, and vengeance. Thus there exists the possibility that the success culture created by the leader may generate its own failure. Only to the extent that the leader is able to temper feelings, to instill enthusiasm in the task at hand, be it ever so menial, and himself continue to reflect an ethical concern—concern about the influence of his actions on the fate of other men—will the organization remain strong and healthy. It is also true that the very strength of the leader may contain the seeds of organizational destruction if changes impinging upon it from outside or the internal organization are brushed aside by him as consisting of so much poppycock.

The leader-manager represents the central force of the organization. To the extent that he assumes for himself the task of planning its course and direction for the future, he becomes involved with change. If he is personally characterized by success based upon earlier experience in a different time, he may be insensitive to the need for personal adjustment and adaptation as the organization moves forward in an environment of internal and external change. The successful manager must be sensitive to changing needs within the organization, as well as to those imposed upon it by changes in the external environment related to technology, markets, or social, political, and economic conditions. He must be recognized as the institutionalized change agent for the organization. He is, therefore, expected to respond to needs that are either structurally determined by innovative activities, or that reflect creativity by the organization's members. In addition, the very creation of an open or closed organization may develop, over time, stress points related to the maintenance of structure, of communication, of acceptance of objectives and goals, or of the various activities required for continued functioning of the organization as a totality.

We thus find another aspect of the leader reflected in what we might refer to as a utopian concern. He must be concerned not only with the future direction of the organization under its charter, but at the same time with the human condition. Besides maintaining standards of effectiveness and efficiency, he must incorporate a deep, personal concern for the kind of organizational world he creates for man within it and for man's life apart from it. By definition, utopias remain ideals. The leader is bound to fall short of the ideal, but he must continue to strive to be a man of vision and compassion meriting the followership of others. As the carrier of organizational values, the leader provides the vision and blows the trumpet so that members may know the course and direction of their collective efforts.

In working toward planned change, the style of leadership governs the implementation of change. If the leader-manager is not able to display the needed adaptability to internal or external requirements, efforts at change will be generated through the rise of alternate centers of power and leadership or by the introduction of change agents from the outside. Both measures have aspects of revolution and usually bring about abrupt change in the existing order.

FOR GOOD TO PREVAIL—SYNERGY

If the leader concurs in the need to expand his openness to experience and to increase his self-awareness, as we suggest, he must alter in positive directions his personal ratio of acceptable to unacceptable interpersonal experience. As we have already seen, the self system is a product of social experience and may be altered by social experience in an environment which allows the individual to safely lower his defenses. In this way he can re-examine and re-evaluate his capacities to meet situations which threaten the essential unity and consistency of his self concept. In this, the leader must take the initiative and develop the programs required for human growth and development.

Let us for a moment stop to consider Pascal's notion that human life is a perpetual illusion. Man is nothing but a disguise, a lie, a hypocrisy, both to himself and in his relationships with others. He does not want others to tell him the truth, and he avoids telling others the truth. All these traits, according to Pascal, far removed from justice and reason, have natural roots in man's heart!

In our Western industrial culture, with its individualistic ideals, there seems to be a greater tendency to depreciate than to appreciate what others have to contribute and what they are. This is the derogatory syndrome, the posture of disdain and disparagement with which we so often confront ideas and sentiments which differ from our own. Its effects are isolation and loneliness, the ultimate expression of a need to be superior. As we manage ourselves and others, we must combat this negative syndrome to build for the future of man.

In looking for ways of expressing superiority, man finds himself weak, however, and tempted to enhance his own status by pulling down others. We in the Western industrialized nations have tended to stress an action orientation. The connotation of inaction is that you are nothing, of action that you are somebody, even though you create this impression by derogating others rather than by being supportive and rising above the crowd on your own merits. This is a cost of democracy which promises each individual that he can rise to the top through individual initiative.

Managers in their leadership role have a critical function to perform in dealing with their superiors, their peers, and their subordinates. It is important to the manager himself as well as to the organization and its members, that he provide organizational and individual conditions conducive to growth and development. As a manager takes his many personal dimensions into account, he will be in a position to increase his interpersonal effectiveness in groups and other organizational relationships. To the extent that he, himself, is able to be open and encourage openness, he can contribute to a general climate of trust and authenticity in the organization. In this way he can best serve the forces of creativity, innovation, and change, relying on synergy as the organization carries out its task and contributes to society's well-being.

SUMMARY

The manager has a unique position in modern society. In a world of science such as ours, permeated by doubt, religious tenets are no longer so persistent as they once were. Consequently, the values provided by managerial leadership assume increasing importance to society. The manager as a transformer must be able to absorb the good and the bad. But in exercising the leadership role, his obligation and his challenge are to transmit only those ideas which can form a constructive base on which to focus the synergy of the members of the organization. He must, therefore, impose upon himself rules of ethical and moral behavior. He must in fact, take the responsibility implicit in knowing that his behavior affects the design of society today and influences the thinking of tomorrow.

We therefore urge managers to move on to the level of need-fulfillment which Maslow calls meta-fulfillment. These terms refer to a spiritual commitment to a productive life orientation. Not only the individual organization, but society itself needs managers and leaders who through physical stamina, intellectual acumen, and ethical and moral concerns are able to hold up the ideals of a generalized good prevailing in man's life. We need to be reminded that even during a period in man's history considered as the Dark Ages, some men were instrumental in the building of cathedrals and the mobilization of men's minds and work to this task.

By being himself synergistic, the manager can create organizations of men mobilized by synergy—in an open adaptive organizational society. Thereby managers and men accept the role of pilot rather than the role of robot and move toward a better world, toward better organizations in which men can live and work.

REFERENCES

Allee, W. C., *Cooperation Among Animals*, New York, Henry Schuman, 1951.

Allport, Gordon W., *The Person in Psychology*, Boston, Beacon Press, 1968.

Ardrey, Robert, *African Genesis*, New York, Dell Publishing, 1961.

Argyris, Chris, *Interpersonal Competence and Organizational Effectiveness*, Homewood, Illinois, Dorsey Press and Richard D. Irwin, 1962.

Barrett, William, *Irrational Man*, Garden City, Doubleday, 1958.

Bennis, Warren G., *Changing Organizations*, New York, McGraw-Hill, 1966.

Bennis, Warren G. *et al*, *Interpersonal Dynamics*, revised edition, Homewood, Illinois, The Dorsey Press, Irwin-Dorsey Ltd., 1968.

Bennis, Warren G. *et al.*, *The Planning of Change*, New York, Holt, Rinehart and Winston, 1961.

Bergson, Henri, *The Two Sources of Morality and Religion*, Garden City, New York, Doubleday, Anchor Book edition, 1935.

Bertalanffy, Ludwig von, *General System Theory*, New York, George Braziller, 1968.

Bion, W. R., *Experiences in Groups*, New York, Basic Books, 1959.

Blau, Peter and W. Richard Scott, *Formal Organizations: A Comparative Approach*, San Francisco, Chandler, 1962.

Brown, J. A. C., *Freud and the Post-Freudians*, Baltimore, Penguin Books, 1961.

Buckley, Walter (Ed.), *Modern Systems Research for the Behavioral Scientist*, Chicago, Aldine, 1968.

Dorsey, John M. and Walter M. Seegers, *Living Consciously: The Science of Self*, Detroit, Wayne State University Press, 1959.

Engel, George L., *Psychological Development in Health and Disease*, Philadelphia, W. B. Saunders, 1962.

Ford, Donald H. and Hugh B. Urban, *Systems of Psychotherapy*, New York, John Wiley and Sons, 1963.

Freud, Sigmund, *Civilization and Its Discontents*, translated by James Strachey, New York, W. W. Norton, first Evergreen edition, 1957.

Freud, Sigmund, *A General Introduction to Psychoanalysis*, New York, Washington Square Press, 1960.

Fromm, Erich, *Escape from Freedom*, New York, Farrar & Rinehart, 1941.

Fromm, Erich, *The Sane Society*, New York, Holt, Rinehart & Winston, 1955.

Hobbes, Thomas, *Leviathan*, Indianapolis, Bobbs-Merrill, The Library of Liberal Arts edition, 1958.

Horney, Karen, *Self-Analysis*, New York, W. W. Norton, 1942.

Iscoe, Ira and Harold Stevenson (Eds.), *Personality Development in Children*, Austin, University of Texas Press, 1960.

Jones, Ernest, *The Life and Work of Sigmund Freud*, Vol. II, New York, W. W. Norton, 1961.

Jourard, Sidney M., *The Transparent Self*, Princeton, D. Van Nostrand, 1964.

Katz, Daniel and Robert L. Kahn, *The Social Psychology of Organizations*, New York, John Wiley & Sons, 1966.

Kluckhohn, Clyde and Henry A. Murray, *Personality in Nature, Society and Culture*, New York, Alfred A. Knopf, 1962.

Laing, R. D., *The Self and Others*, Chicago, Quadrangle Books, 1962.

Lecky, Prescott, *Self-Consistency*, Manden, The Shoestring Press, 1961.

Levinson, Harry, *The Exceptional Executive: A Psychological Conception*, Cambridge, Harvard University Press, 1968.

Locke, John, *The Second Treatise of Government*, New York, The Liberal Arts Press, 1952.

Machiavelli, Niccolo, *The Prince and the Discourses*, New York, Random House, Modern Library edition, 1950.

McGregor, Douglas, *The Human Side of Enterprise*, New York, McGraw-Hill, 1960.

Mann, John, *Changing Human Behavior*, New York, Charles Scribner's Sons, 1965.

Maslow, A. H., *Motivation and Personality*, New York, Harper & Brothers, 1954.

Maslow, A. H., *Toward a Psychology of Being*, Princeton, D. Van Nostrand, 1962.

May, Rollo, *Psychology and the Human Dilemma*, Princeton, D. Van Nostrand, 1967.

Mayo, Elton, *The Human Problems of an Industrial Civilization*, New York, The Viking Press, 1960.

Mayo, Elton, *The Social Problems of an Industrial Civilization*, Boston, Division of Research, Graduate School of Business Administration, Harvard University, 1945.

Menninger, Karl, *The Vital Balance*, New York, The Viking Press, 1963.

Montagu, Ashley, *Man in Process*, New York, New American Library, Mentor edition, 1962.

Perlman, Helen Harris, *Persona—Social Role and Personality*, Chicago, The University of Chicago Press, 1968.

Polanyi, Michael, *The Study of Man*, Chicago, The University of Chicago Press, 1963 edition.

Rogers, Carl, *Client-Centered Therapy*, Boston, Houghton Mifflin, 1951.

Rogers, Carl, *On Becoming a Person*, Boston, Houghton Mifflin, 1961.

Schein, Edgar and Warren Bennis, *Personal and Organizational Change Through Group Methods*, New York, John Wiley and Sons, 1967.

Smith, Adam, *An Inquiry into the Nature and Causes of the Wealth of Nations*, New York, Random House, Modern Library edition, 1937.

Storr, Anthony, *The Integrity of the Personality*, Baltimore, Penguin Books, 1963.

Strauss, Anselm (Ed.), *The Social Psychology of George Herbert Mead*, Chicago, The University of Chicago Press, 1934.

Sullivan, Harry Stack, *The Interpersonal Theory of Psychiatry*, New York, W. W. Nostrand, 1953.

Thompson, Clara, *Psychoanalysis: Its Evolution and Development*, New York, Grove Press, first Evergreen edition, 1957.

Tiryakin, Edward A., *Sociologism and Existentialism*, Englewood Cliffs, N. J., Prentice-Hall, Spectrum edition, 1962.

Waddington, C. H., *The Ethical Animal*, New York, George Allen and Unwin Ltd., 1960.

INDEX

ABCDE7987654321